Organized Labor and Civil Society for Multiculturalism

Organized Labor and Civil Society for Multiculturalism: A Solidarity Success Story from South Korea

BY

JOON K. KIM
Department of Ethnic Studies Colorado State University, USA

emerald
PUBLISHING

United Kingdom – North America – Japan – India – Malaysia – China

Emerald Publishing Limited
Howard House, Wagon Lane, Bingley BD16 1WA, UK

First edition 2020

Reprints and permissions service
Contact: permissions@emeraldinsight.com

British Library Cataloguing in Publication Data
A catalogue record for this book is available from the British Library

ISBN: 978-1-83982-389-3 (Print)
ISBN: 978-1-83982-388-6 (Online)
ISBN: 978-1-83982-390-9 (Epub)

Printed and bound by CPI Group (UK) Ltd, Croydon, CR0 4YY

ISOQAR certified Management System, awarded to Emerald for adherence to Environmental standard ISO 14001:2004.

ISOQAR REGISTERED
Certificate Number 1985
ISO 14001

INVESTOR IN PEOPLE

Table of Contents

List of Tables and Figures

List of Abbreviations

CCEJ	Citizens' Coalition for Economic Justice
CCPR	International Covenant on Civil and Political Rights
CEDAW	Convention on the Elimination of All Forms of Discrimination Against Women
CERD	Convention on the Elimination of All Forms of Racial Discrimination
CESCR	International Covenant on Economic, Social and Cultural Rights
CSO	Civil Society Organizations
EPS	Employment Permit System
ETU-MWD	Equality Trade Union – Migrant Worker Division of Seoul-Kyeongin-Inchon-Area
GongGam	Human Rights Law Foundation (translated from Korean)
ILO	International Labor Organization
IOM	International Organization for Migration
IWRAW	International Women's Rights Action Watch
JCMK	Joint Committee with Migrants in Korea
KCTU	Korean Confederation of Trade Unions
KIC	Korea Institute of Criminology
KIS	Korea Immigration Service
Korea	Republic of Korea or South Korea
KWAU	Korea Women's Associations United
MFA	Migrant Forum in Asia
MINBYUN	Lawyers for a Democratic Society (translated from Korean)
MTU	Migrant Trade Union (Korea)
MWSH	Migrant Worker Struggle Headquarter for Achieving Complete Labor Rights and Actualizing Freedom of Movement and Employment
NGO	Nongovernment Organizations
NOW	National Organization for Women
PSPD	People's Solidarity for Participatory Democracy
UDHR	Universal Declaration of Human Rights
UNHR	United Nations Commission on Human Rights
UNIFEM	United Nations Development Fund for Women (translated from French)

About the Author

Joon K. Kim is a Professor of Ethnic Studies at Colorado State University. Born in Seoul and educated in New York and California, he acquired an academic interest in international migration and multiculturalism in the United States, Korea, and Latin American countries. As a Fellow of the Fulbright Fellowship and the Korea Foundation Field Research, his research focuses on the political economy of immigrant labor, Korea's migrant advocacy and civil society activism, the politics of race via immigration and citizenship, and multicultural education. His strength as a comparative and interdisciplinary scholar is demonstrated by publications in diverse fields and disciplines, including ethnic studies, sociology, history, education, and population studies. His focus on international and comparative labor migrations sprang from his earlier work, "The Political Economy of the Mexican Farm Labor Program, 1942-1964" (*Aztlan: A Journal of Chicano Studies*), which won the ABC-CLIO America: History and Life Award from the Organization of American Historians. He is currently pursuing a new research project on Korean communities of Sao Paulo, Brazil.

Acknowledgments

This book would not have been completed without the support of many people and institutions. First and foremost, I would like to recognize the Association for Foreign Workers' Human Rights in Korea and its past director, Park Seok-Woon, and the present director, Seok Won-Jung, who provided me with invaluable fieldwork experience when I first began research on migrant workers in Korea. My initial field research from 1995 to 1996 was funded by the Fulbright Program, with an institutional affiliation from Seoul National University's Department of Sociology. I would like to extend my thanks to graduate students and professors who supported me during my residence in Seoul.

In 2007–2008, I returned to Korea during my first sabbatical leave. I am indebted to the Korea Foundation Field Research Fellowship for their financial support and to Yonsei University's Korean Studies Program for the institutional affiliation. I am especially grateful to the Program Chair, Professor Kim Hyuk-Rae, for his guidance, generosity, and collaboration. I have also had a tremendous fortune in meeting numerous students and professors while presenting my findings at many institutions in Korea, including Sogang University, Korea University, Seoul National University, Cheongju University, and Changwon University. I extend my appreciation to professors Lee Jung-Hwan and Pyon Bo-Ki for their precious support and friendship. Finally, I am also delighted to serve the Korean Association for Multicultural Education under the leadership of professor Mo Kyung-Hwan, a long-time colleague since our graduate school days, and contribute as an Associate Editor of its journal, the Multicultural Education Review. I appreciate very much the encouragement and collegiality of the editors, professors Cha Yun-Kyung and Lee Moo Sung.

As well, numerous migrant advocacy organizations encouraged my research for the past 25 years. Among many, I am truly grateful to the Joint Committee with Migrants in Korea (JCMK) for providing me with an office space and to its then director, Wu Sam-Yeol, for his enthusiasm and confidence. My volunteer experience at the Korea Migrant Human Rights Center also allowed me to work in collaboration with the then director, Choi Hyun-Mo. Finally, I deeply appreciate all of the other JCMK member organizations, their directors, and, most importantly, to practitioners who work tirelessly in advocating for and solidarity with migrants and their families in Korea.

As my home institution, Colorado State University in Fort Collins has afforded me many opportunities to pursue my research abroad. I would like to express my deep appreciation to the Department of Sociology, my initial department in which I was tenured, and to the Department of Ethnic Studies, my current academic home. Lastly, I am thankful to my department colleagues and to so many other colleagues both in the United States and in Korea for taking part in reviewing my work over the years.

Introduction

While walking across the Sproul Plaza on UC Berkeley campus, I chanced upon a Korean international-student-colleague who showed me a newspaper that featured on its front page a photograph of a man with one of his arms severed. As I read the article, I learned that this man was from Bangladesh and lost his arm working on a press machine in Korea. A question that struck me at the moment was, "How did this man from Bangladesh find himself working in a factory in Korea?" This was the spring of 1994. I was fascinated by this seemingly new development where, for decades, Koreans have gone overseas as laborers and immigrants, not the other way around. I was curious to find out for myself and applied for a research fellowship to study this phenomenon. I landed at Kimpo International Airport in Seoul the following June in 1995, and, since then, I have gone back more than a dozen times to study the evolving changes in Korea's immigrant labor and integration policies.

I was fortunate to secure a visiting graduate-student position at a university in Seoul and quickly figured out a way to meet some of these men from Bangladesh. I volunteered to work for an organization called the Association for Foreign Workers' Human Rights where I met workers from world over, including Pakistan, Myanmar, the Philippines, China, Indonesia, and Bangladesh. My primary work involved listening to various grievances and stories of their work conditions and adaptation to life in Korea. They were from diverse backgrounds; some had been teachers, professionals, and common laborers. Many were single men and women, but there were folks with spouses and children back home. But, in Korea, they shared a common story of abuse working long hours under adverse conditions. Their stories told of egregious violations ranging from passport confiscations and unpaid wages to verbal and physical abuse. My job was to report these cases to the regional labor office where we filed formal complaints against employers.

One day, I met with a group of Pakistani men, with whom we visited the various labor offices, and they invited me to a place of their worship. I learned that it was the holy month of Ramadan, and we took the subway to a city of Itaewon, known for ethnic diversity due to the presence of the US military base in the neighboring city. As we got out of the station and walked through a labyrinth of

Organized Labor and Civil Society for Multiculturalism:
A Solidarity Success Story from South Korea, 1–5

Published under exclusive licence by Emerald Publishing Limited
doi:10.1108/978-1-83982-388-620200011

narrow streets, we were met with literally thousands of non-Koreans walking in one direction. And, suddenly, there appeared a huge, majestic Islamic mosque, which I never knew existed in the middle of the capital city of Seoul. It occurred to me then that this was an amazing sight, thousands of Muslims gathering in one place in a country where such a religion had been virtually unknown. And, immediately, I thought about how they would adapt to life in Korea and how Korea would adjust and evolve with the presence of Muslims and other migrant populations in their midst. This book, in part, seeks to document some of these transformations.

The main context of the changes begins some 30 years ago when Korea experienced a Lewisian turning point, which refers to a transition from labor-exporter to labor-importer, and began a temporary worker program modeled after Japan, Europe, and the United States. Framed as temporary population, the migrants were expected to return to the countries of origin upon fulfilling their economic role. However, this simple idea of repatriating migrants after a few years produced unintended consequences. Many decided to overstay their visas to maximize their earning potential. In short, the state and the labor market structure created conditions conducive of conflicts arising from manufacturing politically vulnerable and ethno racially identifiable population. However, what many of the conflict theorists have failed to consider is the role of civil society organizations in not only protecting and expanding the rights of migrants but also preempting conflicts through their advocacy work.

South Korea stands out among many labor-receiving countries principally because its civil society played a critical role in taking up the struggle to promote labor and citizenship rights of the migrant population. Since its inception, the broad spectrum of civil society organizations unified in opposition to the government's contradictory immigrant labor policies and waged a series of nationwide campaigns, which fostered ideological and cultural linkages among the wider audience by pairing the rights discourse with the plight of immigrant workers. What is most unique about such developments is that the progressive labor unions and labor rights advocates, who had a longstanding experience with labor organizing during the protest movements of the previous decades, spearheaded the labor rights struggles of new immigrant workers. It is difficult to find examples of such demonstration of solidarity between labor unions and immigrant workers anywhere in the world, for the former generally perceives the latter as their competitors who would undermine the labor and living standards. Numerous historical cases illustrate the contrary development has been the norm, where xenophobic rhetoric and antiimmigrant legislations have sprung from labor groups.

Moreover, their consistent advocacy efforts contributed to significant changes in immigration and naturalization policies. The earlier migrant advocacy work quickly spread to other similarly situated population, including the marriage migrants, heritage Koreans from China, Central Asia, and Russia, and the North Korean defectors. Within the past 10 years, the sudden and widespread use of the term *damunhwa* (literally meaning "multiculture") and its attendant policies and practices in government, educational, and private sectors represented an anomaly for a country that has historically exhibited tremendous pride in its presumed homogeneity. The book explains why this transition was possible by tracing the various streams of migrant advocacy movements that successfully structured popular discourse and contributed to the institutionalization of migrant support organizations throughout the country. While started as an advocacy for labor rights of unauthorized workers, the broad spectrum of advocacy organizations and the rising support for diverse migrants greatly expanded the scope of organizations and their work regarding *damunhwa*. The relative few incidents of antiimmigrant movements in South Korea can be attributed to the role of civil society in structuring policies and discourses through their advocacy work since the early 1990s.

Chapter 1, titled "Manufacturing Unauthorized Workers and Advocacy in South Korea," examines the flaws of the industrial trainee system that began in the early 1990s as a way of bringing in workers from overseas. In particular, the chapter highlights the role of nongovernment organizations (NGOs) in their struggle to protect the rights of migrant workers. The successful collaboration of South Korea's civil society stems from its unique historical formation, rooted in democracy movements of earlier decades. More importantly, the role of South Korea's labor unions in advocating for immigrant labor stands out among the traditional countries of immigration, such as the United States and Canada, as well as among its peer nations, such as Japan and Taiwan. Historically, labor unions across the globe have typically perceived immigrant labor as potential competitors who would undermine their labor and living standards. In this regard, this chapter offers a social and political context of South Korea's exceptionalism, with a focus on progressive labor unions and the broad network of civil society organizations in embracing immigrant workers.

Building on their initial accomplishments, Chapter 2 examines the specific policy and legal changes regarding migrant rights by contextualizing the dynamic role of the state, the civil society groups, and the international conventions. While recent scholarship on international migration reflects a growing gap between postnational and state-centered theories, the South Korean case illustrates the dynamic interplay of actors involved in major policy developments concerning immigration and citizenship. South Korea is relatively a newcomer as a labor-receiving country, but the country has experienced a historic change in the Nationality Act and has recently improved the foreign worker policy by implementing the Employment Permit System. Providing the political context of these changes, this chapter shows that the successful outcome of NGO activism depends on the liberal position of the state, the organizational strength of NGOs, and the system of checks-and-balances structurally embedded in the way the state parties and NGOs cooperate in implementing international instruments.

The increased presence of migrant workers in industrial cities of Korea was soon accompanied by feminization of migration. Chapter 3, titled "Sex Workers, Marriage Migrants, and Gender Formation in Migration Advocacy," addresses the two major groups of international women who entered Korea since the mid-1990s. The first group of Russian entertainers and sex workers exemplify the role of race and nationalism in constructing the ideal type of Western women. By contrast, the sudden increase in the number of women "marriage migrants," who intermarried with Korean men predominantly in rural communities, prompted an aggressive effort on the part of the Korean government to speedily assimilate them into the Korean society. While migrant advocacy work generally centered on the precarious political status of industrial trainees who were predominantly males in the manufacturing sector, the influx of foreign women in Korea broadened the scope of public discourse around South Korea's internationalization and revealed layered complexities, one where issues of gender, national identity, race, and power all intersect in various forms of articulations and policies.

As the reliance on migrant populations deepened, the Korean government depended more on overseas heritage Koreans who have grown up in China, Central Asia, and Russia. Each of these Korean emirates and their descendants has a unique history that is tied with the geopolitics of Northeast Asia leading to the establishment of the Korean diasporic communities in these regions. Chapter 4, titled "North Korean Defectors, *Koryoin*, and the Korean Chinese: The Ethnic Question and the Role of Advocacy Organizations," teases out the politicolegal frameworks within which the various Korean heritage migrants entered Korea and the underlying fissures and commonalities that make up these communities in Korea. In their effort to advocate for their respective constituents, the civil society organizations are engaging these Korean heritage communities, reshaping ethnic boundaries, and challenging the essentialist definition of ethno-national identity.

In response to the rapid and significant changes in diversity, the Korean society has quickly adapted to the discourses of multiculturalism. The pace of institutionalizing multicultural education and the scope of support services for multicultural families have been simply unparalleled. While laudable, the projects seeking to promote *damunhwa*, literally translated as multiculture, in South Korea have inadvertently reinforced cultural stereotypes and reproduced cultural hierarchies. Unlike many studies that focus on discrimination against racial or ethnic minority populations, Chapter 5, titled "Internal Orientalism and Multicultural Acts: The Challenges of Multicultural Education in Korea," argues that the seemingly benevolent acts of the majority toward ethnic minority populations in Korea produced unintended consequences. Based on the descriptive content analysis of Internet news stories, this chapter demonstrates the manner in which the dominant Korean society developed an oppositional binary between citizen and foreigner. Building on Edward Said's work, this chapter introduces the concept of *internal Orientalism* that highlights the teleology of cultural distinction by rendering minority populations with weak subjectivity and stigmatizing them as vulnerable populations through a multitude of policies and programs designed to help them. Doing so ironically and simultaneously constructs opportunities for the Korean society to create a benevolent society, thereby crystallizing an interdependent binary between the dominant and minority population.

Chapter 6, titled "From Labor Rights to Multicultural Human Rights: Migrant Advocacy Organizations and Praxis Multiculturalism," examines the central role of the three migrant advocacy umbrella organizations in adapting the language of multiculturalism in their effort to expand the human rights discourse.

Their reliance on various international human rights and labor protocols provided a framework for furthering their advocacy work, but the transition to a discourse that combines multiculturalism with human rights implies a much more critical way of addressing both issues simultaneously. Finally, this chapter introduces the concept of "third-order multiculturalism" that seeks to move beyond the language of diversity by addressing structural and systemic forms of inequality. It calls for ways to reduce social distance across diverse populations, integrate social and cultural spaces through the generic process of everyday life, and diminish the effects of social hierarchy and relative group positions through praxis multiculturalism where the emphasis on individual rights is tempered by a vision of shared responsibility.

Chapter 1

Manufacturing Unauthorized Workers and Advocacy in South Korea

On a wintry day in January 1995, 13 Nepalese workers chained themselves together in front of the historic Myeongdong Cathedral in Seoul to protest Korean government's complicity in abusing international guest workers (J. Kim, 2003; S. Park, 2010; Seok, 2003). Almost two decades later, on January 19, 2014, Cambodians, this time, clamored in front of Bosingak, another landmark in the heart of the bustling Seoul, rebuking the Hun Sen government's violent repression of garment workers who walked off their factories in Phnom Penh (J. Kim, 2015). These two events forecast and testify the struggles and advancement of foreign workers in Korean society. For a country with a great deal of ethnic pride, it would have been difficult to predict then that some 2.5 million foreigners and their Korea-born children would now work, attend schools, and reside in the country.[1] While Korea's demographic change during this period is significant, there are larger stories to be told about the dynamic and complex role of the civil society in not only advocating for the rights of international migrant workers, but also creating conditions for the Korean society to embrace diversity as an integral part of its social fabric.

The introduction of international migrant workers to the Korean society in the early 1990s was a response to the country's changing economic landscape (Fields, 1994; J. Kim, 1996; Y. Park, 1994; Watanabe, 1994). In the late 1980s, Korea had reached the Lewisian turning-point where the country transitioned from labor exporter to labor importer due to major economic developments. In response to the imminent need for labor in declining manufacturing industries, the South Korean government devised a labor-import scheme known as the "Industrial Technical Trainee System" in November of 1991. Since its inception South Korea's trainee system has been replete with problems, reflecting in part the government's inexperience in managing labor import programs as well as its unwillingness to make necessary reforms. Critics of the program argued that the

[1] *Korea Times*, "No. of Foreign Residents in Korea up 8.6% Last Year." Retrieved from http://www.koreatimes.co.kr/www/nation/2019/05/177_269616.html

Organized Labor and Civil Society for Multiculturalism:
A Solidarity Success Story from South Korea, 7–23

Published under exclusive licence by Emerald Publishing Limited
doi:10.1108/978-1-83982-388-620200001

trainee system was tantamount to a "modern-day slavery" because the system was unable to prevent or deal with gross violations of trainees' basic labor and human rights (Korea Research Institute for Workers' Human Rights and Justice, 1995). The first protest led by the Nepalese workers mentioned above targeted the imperfections of the trainee system, particularly in the way the foreign workers were brought in disguised as trainees. Because of their precarious labor status, many trainees fled the companies with which they signed the contracts and became unauthorized workers. The sharp increase in the incidents of trainees-turned-unauthorized-workers ironically activated Korea's civil society (J. Kim, 2003; H. Lee, 2003).

Significant changes began to take place that demonstrated the resiliency of foreign workers and behind-the-scenes advocacy work by civil society. By consistently applying pressure against the government and the consortium of businesses that administer the trainee system, the civil society won a number of notable victories. These included the replacement of the Industrial Technical Trainee System with the Employment Permit System, which provided improved labor condition for the foreign workers; the landmark Supreme Court decision on the Nationality Act that now grants Korean citizenship to children born to mixed heritages; the application of Korea's Labor Standards Law, which now applies to all workers regardless of their political or immigrant status; the government support of more than 200 migrant advocacy and education centers throughout the country; the efforts to align Korea's treatment of migrant workers and other minorities within the parameters of the United Nations human rights instruments; and the embedding of multicultural education through education reforms in the K-12 system and the promotion of diversity through multicultural campaigns. All these efforts collectively helped to transform the politics of culture and curtailed xenophobic violence or antiimmigrant movements in Korea. Despite its relatively brief history, Korea's path to a multicultural society has been paved with sweat and the solidarity vision among the key leaders of its civil society. The difference they collectively made for Korea's multicultural success story is immense and far-reaching; however, it is perhaps even more valuable to appreciate the circumstances and contexts of their advocacy.

International Migrants in Korea's Labor Market

When South Korea's labor shortage in the manufacturing sector peaked at around 11% in the early 1990s, the government initiated a guest worker program modeled after Japan and Germany. Between 1994 and 1997, the government brought in, on average, about 50,000 trainees per year. In the aftermath of the 1997 IMF bailout period, the number of trainees increased significantly to about 145,000 per year between 1998 and 2002 (J. Kim, 2003, p. 244). Importing foreign labor considerably eased the labor shortage situation to around 2% until 2001 (Small and Medium Business Administration (SMBA), 2002). The consistent increase in the number of trainees revealed that the demand for migrant labor had not abated despite the downturns in the economy. One unintended consequence of the trainee system was that it manufactured unauthorized workers as trainees fled the companies in search of better-paying jobs. The primary cause of their job flight was the glaring wage differential between trainees and unauthorized workers since the latter group competed more freely in the labor market and received the prevailing wage. As a consequence, the unauthorized migrant population constituted about 66.2% of the total migrant workers between 1994 and 2003, peaking at 78.4% in 2003 (J. Kim, 2003, p. 246).

In 2007, the Korea Labor Institute published a report on the *Study of Foreign Labor Market Analysis and the Mid-term Assessment of the Management System*, in which it posited that migrants were concentrated in areas where domestic workers shunned and the structural conditions of the domestic labor market would likely induce greater dependence on migrant workers in the foreseeable future. In the manufacturing sector, migrants worked in a variety of areas, but they were disproportionately represented in physically demanding occupations where risks to health were high, such as textile, metal, chemical, and machinery plants (J. Kim, 2009). Also, a great majority of migrants worked in small-to-medium-size companies with less than 100 employees. About half of some 125,000 foreign workers were employed in companies with less than 30 employees, but this number could be considerably higher when unauthorized migrants as well as the figure for companies with fewer than five employees are taken into consideration. As years progressed, migrants began to move into construction, agriculture, and restaurant and lodging services. The report revealed a considerable wage gap between national and foreign workers in industries where foreigners were overrepresented, such as electronics, manufacturing, certain service sectors (restaurants, lodging – motels, inns, and hotels), and construction industries. Foreigners earned about 4,000 won per hour relative to 5,600 won for domestic workers, and the total wage increased to about 4,820 won for foreign workers when accommodation costs were added. More importantly, a significant wage gap also existed between legally employed foreigners and unauthorized migrants, who made 84.4% and 94.7% of domestic worker earnings, respectively. The comparisons were based on similar occupations between domestic and migrant workers.

These general trends of migrant employment partly explain domestic labor employment patterns. It appears that more and more young men and women are turning away from jobs that now foreigners occupy, thus perpetuating the labor shortage situation in 3-D (dirty, dangerous, and difficult) occupations. Among domestic workers, the average age of employees in key sectors increased significantly between 1985 and 2005. In electronics, for instance, the average age was 29.2 in 1985 as compared to 41.9 in 2005. Similar increases in manufacturing (27.7 in 1985 and 39.7 in 2005), construction (34.2 in 1985 and 41.8 in 2005), and restaurant and lodging (34.9 in 1985 and 44.6 in 2005) sectors demonstrate a major shift in occupation preference among young people in Korean society. Moreover, during the same period, domestic workers with low-skilled and high-skilled levels increased in small-to-mid and large size companies, respectively. Because foreign workers are generally hired in smaller companies, the negative hiring trends of the bigger companies indicate a potential gap in filling these positions, especially those who have three years or more of work experience in the same line of work. These indicators indirectly suggest that the actual displacement of domestic workers has not occurred as a result of importing foreign labor and that the critical needs exist in recruiting additional experienced labor or attracting domestic workers. In the restaurant and lodging businesses, the high employment rate suggests a major shift in employee preference for these jobs in companies that hire more than 10 employees.

The structure of labor market for foreigners is actively buttressed by state policies that impose a legal framework for labor migration, employment conditions, migrant mobility, and residency. Since the beginning of migrant import programs, the government has closely managed the migrant labor population. From the initial industrial trainee system to the present Employment Permit System, the government's position on low-skilled international workers has been clear. Migrants were expected to return to the countries of origin upon completion of their work in Korea. This simple idea, however, produced many unintended consequences, including the creation of unauthorized migrant population, the continued labor shortage and dependence on low-wage international workers, and the long-term settlement of migrants. Some migrants returned home as the government had anticipated, but many more came to Korea and established their roots because of the sustained dependence on foreign workers.

Activation of Civil Society[2]

The temporary labor importation scheme designed to send international workers back to the countries of their origin upon completion of their work unexpectedly generated unauthorized workers and activated South Korea's civil society. Several highly publicized incidents prompted the formation of migrant advocacy organizations. On November 10, 1993, Ho Lim, an ethnic Korean from China, committed suicide by jumping off an overpass in the busy intersection near Seoul Youngdeungpo District Office. He had arrived in Korea in May 1992 with an older sister, Haesun, and a younger brother Joong-ho, on a family visitation visa.[3] They had been farmers in China, but the stories of their neighbors becoming rich by working in Korea piqued their interest. Their decision to visit Korea cost them about 6,000 yuan (US$1,000), but they were hopeful that by working hard

[2]The phrase was used by Su-Hoon Lee (1993) in order to describe the transitional period in politics from an authoritarian regime to the first democratically elected president during the period between 1987 and 1992 when an unprecedented number of NGOs emerged in the Korean society.

[3]After the 1988 Seoul Olympics, the Korean government initiated a program to reunite families that were split up during the Korean War. Many Koreans had also fled to China and settled in northern and northeastern border towns at the end of the nineteenth century. They were forcibly recruited to aid the Japanese during the expansionist period immediately after the establishment of the puppet state of Manchukuo in 1932. After Japan's defeat in WWII, some 1.1 million ethnic Koreans who could not return to Korea or chose to stay in China were eligible to visit Korea.

and saving diligently they would return to China with enough savings to buy a car. After working in various construction sites for a year, he had decided to go back to China by reporting to an immigration office in Mokdong, Seoul. Upon paying the exorbitant fine (US$1,900) for overstaying his visa and purchasing the boat fare (US$900), he only had US$135 left in his possession. Disappointed and heartbroken, he ended his life on the asphalt pavement in Seoul (J. Song, 2006, p. 34).

Shortly after the incident, a series of on-the-job accidents exemplified the intrinsic problems of the trainee system. The lack of adequate trainee education, combined with the concentration of migrant workers in 3-D occupations, generated numerous accidents and health problems. More importantly, as trainees, they were exempted from Korea's Labor Standards Law, which meant that they were technically not considered "workers," thus denied medical coverage and other labor protections. As the number of job-related accidents climbed to new heights, several leaders emerged as the moral figure who brought the plight of migrant workers to the national spotlight. In a highly visible demonstration, some fifteen migrant workers waged a sit-in protest from January 9 to February 7, 1994, at Citizens' Coalition for Economic Justice (CCEJ).[4] The Reverend Seo Kyung-Seok, who has been touted as Korea's Ralph Nader and who co-founded CCEJ five years earlier, promulgated the government's failure to recognize the egregious violations of labor and human rights of migrant workers. Shortly thereafter, President Kim Young-sam announced a plan to provide medical coverage for all foreign workers regardless of their immigration status, and, in September 1994, the government handed down a directive that commissioned the Ministry of Labor to adjudicate all cases involving labor rights violations involving foreign workers (S. Park, 2010). The successful campaigning emboldened the base of the migrant advocacy organizations and sparked a wave of additional protests calling for an expansion of labor rights to trainees and unauthorized workers.

As the stories of foreign workers gained national prominence, the advocacy organizations consolidated their efforts into a central organization. Another Protestant minister, Kim Hae-sung,[5] who began his ministry among the factory workers in the city of Sungnam in the mid-1980s, founded the Sungnam City Human Rights

[4]The organization was formed in July 1989 on the principle of sustaining a fair market order and achieving economic justice. It represents one of the first progressive national citizens' movement organizations that emerged in the late-1980s in Korea. CCEJ departs significantly from the more radical minjung movement organizations in that the focus is peaceful social change through nonviolence, legal means, and policy changes (Wells, 1995).

[5]In his early career, the Reverend Kim was inspired by the work of his predecessor and mentor, the Reverend Lee Hae-hak, who was a prominent leader of the National Council of Churches and an advocate of minjung theology, a critical branch of pro-democracy movements during the military governed, dictatorial regimes of the 1970s and 1980s. The Reverend Lee had been the minister of the Sungnam Jumin (Citizens) Church.

Committee of the National Council of Churches and established the "Support Center for Foreign Worker Human Rights" primarily for the Korean Chinese who poured into the city in the late-1980s (H. Kim, 1998). The Reverend Kim emerged as a national leader for migrant workers when he was selected as the inaugural co-representative of the organization, the Joint Committee with Migrant Workers in Korea (JCMK). This umbrella body would serve as the administrative headquarter of more than forty migrant-advocacy organizations, which ranged from labor counseling centers and religious organizations to mutual aid associations and labor unions. Formed in June 1995, JCMK's initial goal was to introduce a bill titled "Foreign Worker Protection Law." This bill sought to create Foreign Workforce Policy Committee, consisting of diverse constituents in various government and nongovernment sectors, through which it would provide policy recommendations and sought to institute robust labor protection measures for all migrant workers. The bill's ultimate goal was to replace the trainee system with a work permit system whereby foreign workers would be treated more or less the same way as domestic workers, with an ability to renew their permits every five years (C. Park, 2019).

The centralized structure of the advocacy organizations not only facilitated communication but also enabled a unified vision among the diverse constituents. Since its launch, JCMK consistently framed the migrant stories from a human rights perspective, emphasizing the need to "protect" foreign workers against discrimination and to foster their inalienable rights as both laborers and people. Significantly, the human rights discourse coincided with three interrelated events that unfolded in the latter part of the 1990s and into the next decade: the presidential election of a former political dissident, Kim Dae-Jung, who had all his life championed "universalism and globalism" as reflected in the United Nation's Universal Declaration of Human Rights (J. Kim, 2005); the establishment of National Human Rights Commission of Korea in 2001; and the NGO participation in both international migrant labor solidarity networks and UN-based human rights conventions. The political liberalization under President Kim accelerated the pace of social change in Korea, aligning itself with international standards for how migrants and their families ought to be treated. Some of the core Korean NGO groups, such as People's Solidarity for Participatory Democracy, the Lawyers for Democratic Society, and Sarangbang Center for Human Rights, among others, worked in concert with JCMK in numerous international forums and conferences, and they collectively worked on ways to bring Korea in alignment with international standards as reflected in the various human rights instruments to which South Korea is a signatory, including International Covenant on Economic, Social and Cultural Rights; International Covenant on Civil and Political Rights; Convention on the Rights of the Child; Convention on the Elimination of All Forms of Discrimination against Women; and International Convention on the Elimination of All Forms of Racial Discrimination (J. Kim, 2005, p. 408). In 1998, for instance, JCMK, in the Philippines, co-participated to promote and ratify the UN Convention on the Protection of the Rights of All Migrant Workers and Members of their Families. The organizations that supported such effort from Korea represent a wide array of interests and provide the international solidarity networks with valuable information and insights from their respective fields.[6]

The migrant advocacy work rooted in human rights discourse greatly diversified the network participants and widely promoted the plight of migrant workers throughout Korea. By the end of the 1990s, some 150 migrant support and advocacy organizations had formed, with many providing labor-related support-services. The Protestant and Catholic churches, however, operationalized a different framework than the rights-based discourse on which many advocacy organizations depended. In an interview with the Reverend Kim Hae-sung, he confided that what migrants needed were not money or rights as much as the Good News. He came to this realization after having fought for and won a significant amount of compensation from a company where a migrant worker had lost his wrist. Some months later, this worker from Bangladesh wrote to the Reverend Kim proudly claiming that he was able to find another wife upon his return to his homeland even though he had been already married with children (H. Kim, 1998). Combining mission and outreach, the church leaders framed the migrant worker issues in the context of the biblical message and rapidly expanded their organizational capacity. Whether seen as strangers or gentiles, the migrants came to represent a new population in need of church's support and God's message (Byun, 2001; S. Park, 2002). Inspired by the gospel's liberation message, the Korean Presbyterian Church established the Foreign Worker Counseling Center in Ansan, where foreign worker population is heavily concentrated in the city's two major industrial complexes, in order to "proclaim freedom for the prisoners and recovery of sight for the blind, [and] to release the oppressed." Other church organizations followed suit and became a part of the sudden counseling explosion within the past five years. Reverend Lee Cheol-woo of the Kwangju Foreign Worker Mission Center, for instance, proclaimed God's command to "love those who are aliens," suggesting that foreign workers are like the Jews exiled in Egypt.

There is, however, a clear distinction between the progressive or activist Protestant ministers who espouse the minjung theology – a Korean version of liberation theology (D. Kim, 2011) and the conservative churches whose primary purpose is to proselytize migrant populations. While some of the Catholic nuns and priests provided important support services for migrants, many were not particularly on the forefront of advocating for migrant rights. Regardless, by the early 2000s, the number of Protestant and Catholic churches providing some combination

[6]These organizations include the following: Pax Romana, Citizen Network for Cultural Reform, Council for Representatives of Health Care Organizations, Green Korea United, Joint Committee for Migrant Workers in Korea, Korea Confederation of Trade Unions, Korean Federation for Workers' Safety and Health, Korea Center for City and Environment Research, Korean Peoples' Artists Federation, Korea Teachers' and Educational Workers' Union, Korea Women's Association United, Lawyers for Democratic Society, National Association of Professors for Democratic Society, People's Solidarity for Participatory Democracy, People's Solidarity for Social Progress, Research Institute for the Handicapped Rights in Korea, SARANGBANG Group for Human Rights, Struggle Network for Migrant Workers' Labor Rights and Freedom of Migration.

of mission work and various support services increased in significant numbers principally because of the manner in which migrants had been framed as a vulnerable population deserving of empathy, support, and protection.

Framing Migrant Issues: Mass Media and Public Perception

The continuing advocacy of church leaders established an ethical and biblical framework that conveyed sympathy and concern for migrants, rather than a threat to the public in economic or cultural terms. Numerous television programs, in which key church leaders frequently appeared, featured special topics on migrant struggles and difficulties, the debates about the prospect of multiculturalism, and the contributions of migrants to the Korean society. Riding on the wave of these widely circulated stories, two mainstream television networks aired specials about marriage migrants and their families on a weekly basis during primetime. The first was *Love in Asia*, which featured the lives of particularly women migrants who have married Korean men in rural communities. The general tenor of the message was simple: that women migrants are making an important contribution to society, and they are struggling to adjust to new culture and life in the communities and society. The second show, *In-Laws: Nice to Meet You*, addressed a similar theme as *Love in Asia*, but it brought the parents of interethnic couples together by inviting in-laws to Korea and by exchanging televised messages between families. These communications often generated interest and participation from the entire communities.

Both of these shows demonstrated skillfully the human aspects of migration and contributed to more wholistic images of migrants. Aside from these television shows, mainstream newspaper columns consistently framed migrant issues in sympathetic terms. An analysis of news coverage during this period revealed three dominant themes: migrants faced tremendous difficulties in the process of attaining the Korean dream; migrant support efforts were highly encouraged and celebrated; and migrants were transforming Korea into a multicultural society.[7] Described as a disadvantaged minority, migrants were often depicted as victims of unfair treatment. In a fire at the Yeosu Immigration Detention Center on February 11, 2007, ten detained migrants died and 17 more incurred serious injuries. These migrant deaths demonstrated powerfully how their hope of fulfilling the Korean dream could turn into a nightmare and showed symbolically the woefully inadequate protection for migrants. In an opinion column, angry voices filled the pages:

> Not only did the fire that day take away the lives of migrant workers, but also it showed to the rest of the world a reflection of those ugly, blemished faces of people who exploit them.[8]

---

[7]This news story analysis was based on a review of articles that appeared in one-year period between February 2007 and February 2008. There was a total of 120 articles from major news outfits, but it excluded articles that were from the peripheral cities and provinces. Aside from only a few articles, the vast majority of the stories sympathized with migrants.

[8]Ko, Mi-Sook, "A Nation of Exploitation" [*Ppingttang tteutneun nara*], *Kyunghyang Shinmun*, March 19, 2007, p. 31.

Other heartbreaking stories about unauthorized migrants appeared regularly in newspapers, including those who incurred industrial accidents,[9] fell victim to violence and abuse,[10] and perished tragically.[11]

The stories about these unfortunate events were counterbalanced by equally powerful and uplifting messages concerning migrant support activities. Highlighting individuals who were making notable contributions, newspapers reported a flurry of activities promoting general welfare of migrants, emphasizing people's proclivity to do good works, and enhancing positive relations. Some of the good-will gestures included free medical services, free driving lessons for women migrants, collecting books from overseas travelers for migrants, financial support of a school for Mongol children, and establishment of internet broadcast station for migrants.[12] In celebration of special holidays and occasions, there were plenty of reports about people extending goodwill toward migrants and spreading kindness.[13] The following newspaper headlines captured the spirit of their

[9]Chon, Jin-Shik, "The Severed Hand and Foot of Korean Dream ... Never Dreamed of an Industrial Accident," *Hankyureh*, March 24, 2007, p. 6.

[10]See the articles: Choi, Sang-won, "Foreign Worker in Serious Condition after a Beating," *Hankyureh*, June 29, 2007, p. 9; Lee, Jae-Myung, "A Man Flees Hospital during Treatment Fearing Exposure of Unauthorized Status," *Hankyureh*, March 19, 2007, p. 9.

[11]A 49-year-old Thai worker was suffering from severe stomach pains but refused to go to hospital for a fear of being deported; his Thai friends discovered him on Christmas Day and promptly took him to a nearby hospital, but it was to no avail. He died the following day. *See* the article by Lee, Cheon-yeol, "A Migrant Dies Unable to Pay for a Surgery" [*Ijunodongja byungwonbi eopseo samang*], *Seoul Shinmun,* December 31, 2007. Another fire accident at an ice box storage in Ichon, Kyunggi Province, took away the lives of thirteen ethnic Korean from China and a Uzbekhistani worker. Their tragic deaths were compounded by the inadequate insurance coverage by the company employer. *See* Hwang, Il-Song, "Sadness Follows a Migrant Even After His Death" *Kukminilbo,* 8 January 2008. Another migrant dies trying to flee from an immigration officer. *See* Kim, Yeon-Ki, "A Migrant Dies Trying to Evade a Crackdown," *Hankyureh,* January 17, 2008, p. 12.

[12]See the articles: Kim, Se-Dong, "Eunpyung County – Resident Foreigners Give-and-Take: Reciprocating Free Medical Treatment with Volunteer Work," *Munhwailbo*, April 18, 2007, p. 13; "Free Medical Service for Migrant Workers," *Kukminilbo*, June 28, 2007, p. 18; "A Small Miracle from a Hospital for Migrant Workers," *Hankyureh*, July 25, 2007, p. 27; Jeong, Hyuk-Soo, "Chungnam Province Police, Free Driver's Education Invites Huge Response from Women Marriage Migrants," *Kyunghyang Shinmun*, August 29, 2007, p. 10; Kwon, Bok-Ki, "A Campaign for Collecting Books Written in Migrants' Language," *Hankyureh*, September 18, 2007, p. 22; Park, Jae-Chan, "A Good Samaritan Pays for School Facility for the Mongol Children," *Kukminilbo*, September 20, 2007, p. 25; Lee, Moon-Yeong, "Internet Broadcasting Station Opens for Migrants," *Seoul Shinmun*, December 11, 2007, p. 20.

[13]*See* Choi, Sang-Won, "Scarred by a Korean, Let Us All Help toward Healing," *Hankyureh*, July 19, 2007, p. 13; Park, Jae-Chan, "In this Lunar New Year ... Toward a Celebration of Sharing and Serving," *Kukminilbo*, September 19, 2007, p. 2; "End-of-Year Fundraising for Migrants," *Seoul Shinmun*, November 8, 2007, p. 23; Kim, Seok-Jong,

support: "We are All Neighbors: Colorful Christmas Celebration" (*Kyunghyang Shinmun*, December 24, 2007), "Protecting Migrant Human Rights with a Complementary System Change" (*Kukminilbo*, May 1, 2007), "Extending the Basic Rights to Migrants Equally" (*Hankyureh*, August 31, 2007), "Memorial Service for Yeosu Fire Victims: To Heaven where Discrimination Does not Exist" (*Kukminilbo*, March 31, 2007), "'Subway No. 1 Line': The Musical Running Together with Our Alienated Neighbors" (*Hankukilbo*, August 10, 2007), and "Hospitals for the Society's Disadvantaged Expand" (*Hankyureh*, August 13, 2007). Collectively, these heartfelt news reports greatly offset the tragic ones and contribute to positive orientation toward migrants.

While the media arguably played a critical role in shaping public attitude, a vast majority of Koreans did not interact with migrants on a daily basis. In order to gauge the level of receptivity concerning migrants among Koreans, the Korea Women Development Institute (KWDI, 2004), under the auspice of the Ministry of Gender Equality and Family, conducted a national study (n=2,000) about public perception and attitude toward migrants. The results of the study confirmed and reflected the general media messages. The overwhelming majority (78.1%) of the survey respondents expressed a concern that migrants faced discrimination, and more than a third (34.6%) of the respondents believed migrants' experience with discrimination to be very serious. In contrast, a negligible number (5.8%) of respondents showed that migrants had not experienced discrimination at all. In terms of the age distribution of respondents, people in thirties expressed the seriousness of discrimination the most, followed closely by those in the twenties and forties. The older respondents over the age of 50 reflected this general pattern, but they were less likely than the younger cohorts to say that discrimination was very serious. This was significant, though not surprising, given that the younger generation may be more attuned to migrant issues, while the older generation may have a higher level of tolerance for discrimination. There was also a notable difference across economic class and educational attainment levels. People who earned more than 4 million won (approximately US$4,300 per month) and those who have at least high school diplomas empathized more with the migrant situation than the rest. On a different question, the respondents were asked to identify how they formed perception about migrants. Almost nine-out-of-ten (89%) respondents pointed to mass media, such as newspapers, television, and radio programs. Needless to say, the media was perhaps the most important window through which Koreans identified with migrant issues.

In assessing public attitude toward migrants in diverse areas of work and life, the majority of the responses confirmed the perception that migrants were unfairly treated and, therefore, implied such treatments should be stopped or avoided.

"We are All Neighbors: Colorful Christmas Celebration," *Kyunghyang Shinmun*, December 24, 2007, p. 24; Park, Eun-Kyung, "Radio Star: Wooden Bicycle – 'Wishing it could become a Ray of Hope for Migrants,'" *Kyunghyang Shinmun*, January 14, 2008.

In the area of work and employment, the majority (56.6%) of the respondents clearly opposed granting opportunities to migrants only in areas where domestic workers shunned. About one-in-eight (12.5%) persons expressed an agreement with the statement. On a more general question about whether migrants should be treated equally as domestic workers, the affirmative responses (21.8%) were highest for this question. Although this question did not clearly articulate the content of treatment, it reflected opinion of a significant portion of the population who implicitly considered differential treatment to be acceptable. Similarly, 21.3% and 20.9% of the respondents held views that migrants were more suitable for simple, manual labor and that their productivity level fell short of the national standard, respectively. On the question that measured a social distance between migrants and Korean nationals, a significant number of people (18%) agreed with the statement that migrants should live among themselves. These responses suggested two important developments: first, the majority of Koreans felt sympathy toward migrants who were filling important needs in the economy and social life, and, second, migrants were not yet viewed as potential citizens on equal terms as Koreans.

Advocacy Outcomes and Social Change

The sudden expansion and diversification of migrant advocacy networks contributed to the popular perception that foreign workers provided necessary labor in niche economies but endured hardships and discrimination. The broad scope of organizations and their combined social strength to influence public opinion culminated in foreign worker policy amendments and yielded notable societal changes. These transformations can be divided into the following categories: improvements in basic labor rights, formation of benevolent or mutual aid associations, expansion of government-financed migrant support centers, and a historic Supreme Court decision on an anachronistic National Law.

The advancement in basic labor rights of foreign workers occurred in succession through consistent efforts of the advocacy organizations (Table 1.1). The first significant victory for the migrant workers occurred shortly after the Nepalese demonstration. On September 15, 1995, the Supreme Court of Korea ruled that the application of Korea's Labor Standards Law to foreigners did not depend on their legal status. While the immigration law prohibited unauthorized residency of foreigners, it did not nullify their labor rights as guaranteed by the Labor Standards Law. Article 33 of the Constitution further stipulated *sam-kwon* (or "three rights") that laborers shall possess freely "the right of organization, the right of collective bargaining, and the right of collective action." This decision was significant because some 60% of 103,000 foreign workers had already become unauthorized workers by the end of 1995. Moreover, it allowed the trainees to receive compensation for on-the-job accidents. Between 1995 and 2000, accident victims received over 29.6 billion won (approximately $29.6 million). In 1998 alone, the Labor Ministry reported that foreign workers incurred 755 industrial accidents, of whom there were 35 deaths (Korea Labor Welfare Corporation, 2003).

Table 1.1. Chronology of NGO Activism.

Date	Organization	Content
October 26, 1991	Ministry of Justice Order No. 255	Foreign trainees employed by Korean companies located overseas began entering Korea based on "Foreign Industrial Trainee Visa Issuance and related Instructions"
June 1992	Ministry of Justice	Due to escalating demand for foreign labor and the preponderance of unauthorized workers, the Government announces the amnesty program. From June 1992 to May 1994, the Government extended the amnesty program four times
January 1, 1994	Ministry of Justice Order No. 294	Foreign Industrial Trainee Program initiated; Small and Medium Business Administration administers 27 manpower recruiting agencies; trainees recruited from 11 countries
February 1994	CCEJ	Fourteen foreign workers gather in the auditorium of the Citizens' Coalition for Economic Justice (CCEJ) protesting the government's inadequate protection for the victims of industrial accidents. A foreign worker had incurred on-the-job accident and died
March 1994	Ministry of Justice	Industrial Accident Insurance applies to undocumented workers
September 1994	Ministry of Justice	Retroactively applies industrial accident compensation up to three years to foreign workers who had already returned to their countries of origin
January 9, 1995	Nepalese protest	Thirteen Nepalese industrial trainees protest in Seoul, demanding changes in the Foreign Industrial Trainee System
February 14, 1995	Ministry of Labor Order No. 258	Announces the implementation of the Minimum Wage Law and the Labor Standard Law to foreign industrial trainees
June 1995	JCMK	Foreign worker counseling centers establish a central organization under the name, the Joint Committee for Migrant Workers in Korea
September 16, 1995	Supreme Court	Renders a decision permitting unauthorized workers to receive industrial accident compensation, stating that "the immigration laws regulate and prohibit employment of unauthorized immigrants but do not have the enforcement authority to nullify labor rights of those who are already employed"

Table 1.1. *(Continued)*

Date	Organization	Content
October 1995	JCMK	Initiates a month-long event for improving the human rights of foreign workers begins with a celebration at Yonsei University; officially establishes October as the "foreign workers' month"
July 1996	JCMK	Jointly sponsors with Asian Migrant Center (Hong Kong) and Migrant Forum in Asian (MFA) an international conference called "Migrant Workers Challenging Global Structures" in Seoul
October 1996	JCMK	Protests in front of the National Assembly building; requests a legislative adoption of the "Foreign Worker Protection Law" in the National Assembly and submits 56,512 signatures in support of the law
July 1997	JCMK	Begins a hunger strike in support of the "Foreign Worker Protection Law" in Myung-dong, Seoul
October 1997	Supreme Court	According to the Labor Standard Law, the Court establishes that unauthorized foreign workers should be paid retirement pay
March 11, 1998	Ministry of Justice	Announces a slight revision of the Foreign Industrial Trainee Program, allowing foreign trainees two years of training followed by one year of regular employment
December 9, 1998	JCMK	Campaigns for the ratification of the UN convention on the "Protection of the Rights of All Migrant Workers and Members of their Families" in the Philippines
September 21, 1999	MUMK	Establishes the Medical Mutual-Aid Union for Migrant Workers in Korea (MUMK)
April 2000	KLAC	The Seoul Bar Association forms a legal counseling service called, Korea Legal Aid Corporation (KLAC), for foreign workers
May 2000	JCMK	Organizes a workshop on foreign worker employment and the Employment Permit System
November 2000	JCMK	Organizes a hunger strike for the promotion of foreign worker human rights from November 27 to December 6. A petition containing 500 signatures calling for the elimination of discrimination against foreign workers and for the protection of their rights was printed in national newspaper, *Hankyoreh*

Table 1.1. *(Continued)*

Date	Organization	Content
December 2000	JCMK	Sponsors Foreign Worker Tenth Anniversary Photo History
June 2001	JCMK	Participates in the Seventh Regional Conference on Migrants and the Second MFA (Migrant Forum in Asia) Conference
December 2001	JCMK	Publishes "White Paper on Migrant Workers' Human Rights," detailing in its 320-page report numerous human rights infringement cases against foreign workers and an alternative to the existing Industrial Technical Trainee Program
January 2002	Foreign workers protest	Ninety-seven foreign workers end a sit-in strike at a furniture factory in Pochon. The workers from Russia, Uzbekistan, Iran, Nigeria, Rumania, the Philippines, Thailand, Mongolia, and Moldavia protest against nonpayment of wages and verbal abuses by Korean staff at the company. Majority of the protesters are undocumented
February 2002	Korea Human Rights Commission	Sixteen undocumented workers file a petition with the Human Rights Commission to reclaim some 50 million won in delayed wages. They are farm workers in reclaimed land on Ganghwa Island, Inchon. Lee Yong-seok, a Yonsei University Professor, has been helping the petitioners
March 2002	Ministry of Justice	Announces an amnesty period from March 25 to May 29 for unauthorized foreign residents
April 2002	JCMK	Holds a press conference on abolishing the Trainee-Employment System
June 2002	JCMK	Holds a joint forum for improving foreign worker rights with Japan (Korean Human Rights Commission)
July 2002	JCMK	Begins a series of protests, press conferences, and hunger strikes calling for the eradication of the industrial trainee system and expressing opposition to the forced repatriation of unauthorized foreign workers. Some 52 foreign worker counseling centers jointly initiated the protest, and the movement spread to other major cities including Taegu, Jeonju, Inchon, Bucheon, Ansan, Kwangju (Kyunggi), and Pusan

Table 1.1. *(Continued)*

Date	Organization	Content
September 2002	COCATS	Common Committee for Opposing Crackdown on Migrant Workers, Abolition of Trainee System and Securing Migrants' Rights, Korea (COCATS), an umbrella organization of 166 foreign worker advocacy groups, holds an inauguration ceremony for "Defenders of Human Rights for Foreign Workers" in Myeong-dong, Seoul. In addition, 20 other human rights groups from 10 countries announce the "Peace Declaration for Asian Migrant Worker Human Rights"
October 2002	Bucheon Counseling Center	Bucheon Foreign Workers' House celebrates its third annual foreign worker festival at the Bucheon Jungang (Central) Park; some 10,000 workers representing over 10 nationalities are expected to participate
October 2002	MUMK	Korean doctors with over 600 participating hospitals establishes "The Medical Mutual-Aid Union for Migrant Workers (MUMK)," a medical insurance system for the nation's 300,000 foreign workers. The plan already drew over 10,000 subscribers, most of whom are undocumented workers
November 2002	Smile Welfare Foundation	Over 100 dentists came together and formed the Smile Welfare Foundation, providing free dental surgery and other treatments to the disabled, low-income families, and foreign workers
November 22, 2002	Korean Human Rights Commission	Sponsors Korea-Japan NGO Forum, "Diverse Ethnicities Crossing Borders: Experiencing Multicultural Living"
April 20, 2003	JCMK	Participates in the KBS TV special on the Employment Permit System; 100 people participated in the discussion.
June 29, 2003	FKTU	The Federation of Korean Trade Unions sponsors a mass meeting calling for the eradication of the Industrial Trainee System and for the implementation of the Labor Permit System
July 31, 2003	National Assembly	Passes the "Foreign Worker Employment-Related Law"

Source: Originally published in the study by J. Kim (2005, pp. 402–405).

Buoyed by the recent Supreme Court decision, the well-coordinated civil society organizations galvanized their efforts around the passage of the Foreign Worker Protection Law (Seol, 2000). In preparation for the submission of the draft law to the National Assembly, JCMK and church organizations took their grievances to the streets, collecting some 120,000 signatures in fall 1996. In the following summer, 78 organizations formed the Central Committee for the Passage of the Foreign Worker Law (J. Song, 2006, pp. 34–36). While this bill would be stalled for another two years due to the intense opposition by the business leaders, other important developments bolstered the support for and status of migrant workers. The increasing cases of industrial accidents and job-related health problems among foreign workers prompted many of these organizations to establish medical mutual-aid organizations. In September 1999, medical professionals and volunteers formed a network of doctors, clinics, and other support organizations, in order to provide centralized information for foreign workers and offer low-cost or free medical services. Between 1999 and 2002, these hospitals supported up to 50% of the costs for 628 cases of hospitalization, surgery, child delivery, and emergency care, amounting to about 257 million won (US$ 257,000) (Medical Network, 2002). These NGOs' emphasis on the basic human rights of foreign workers garnered widespread public support. It is simply astounding that, within a span of five years, over 150 independent organizations emerged in order to assist foreign workers on a range of issues, including nonpayment of wages, industrial accidents, physical abuse, residency status, repatriation, and interethnic marriages.

On December 13, 1997, the Supreme Court of Korea echoed the public sentiment regarding the precarious political status of migrants by ruling the Nationality Act unconstitutional. Prior to its fourth revision, the Nationality Act stipulated that a child born between a Korean mother and a foreign father assumed the citizenship status of the father. Although this decision was a product of the foregoing efforts on the part of women's movement groups that persisted for changes in the Family Law, the revised citizenship law reflected a major turning point in Korea's ethnic history. This remarkable decision buttressed government's consistent support of interethnic marriages in Korea. While the changes in the Nationality Act promoted gender equality broadly, the new government initiative that supported multicultural families speaks to gender imbalance in rural communities where there existed a severe shortage of marriageable women. Since the mid-1990s, the local governments and privately owned marriage consulting firms have joined hands in promoting interethnic marriages between rural Korean men and women from various countries in Southeast Asia, China, the Philippines, Central Asia, and Russia. With significant increases in such marriages over the next decade, the National Assembly passed two laws that established a legal basis for supporting multicultural families. The first law, titled "the Basic Law Concerning the Treatment of Foreigners in Korea" (hereafter Basic Law), articulated new policy designs and structures by charging the Ministry of Justice with the responsibility of devising a basic foreigner policy.[14] In the following year, the National Assembly again passed the "Multicultural Family Support Law," intended to foster stability and social integration of multicultural families. The specifics of the programs included cultural educational opportunities, family counseling focused on mediating cultural conflicts, and language acquisition programs for both children and a foreign parent. In order to deliver these programs, the Ministry of Health, Welfare, and Family Affairs was authorized to operate more than 100 multicultural family support centers nationwide (J. Kim, 2011, p. 1594).

The historic decision on citizenship and the promotion of interethnic marriages created new dilemmas for which the Korean society had not adequately prepared. By the mid-2000s, Korea's foreigner population surpassed the one-million mark and some 35,000 interethnic marriages constituted 13.6% of total marriages in Korea (J. Kim, 2011, p. 1595). Of these populations, the children of interethnic marriages accounted for 12% (or 168,583 persons), many of whom have matriculated into the public-school systems. The challenge of dealing with diversity in classrooms turned into a new area of concern for many advocacy centers as well as for teachers and educators broadly as they needed to grapple with the task of educating students about what it means to live in a diverse environment, something for which they had little to no training. Initially, the advocacy centers sought to bring "diversity curriculum" into the classrooms by recruiting migrant workers who introduced various cultural artifacts, such as clothes, foods, and other products that students would be able to touch, taste, and experience. Such a fetishizing method of introducing culture to the Korean population was a common practice from numerous cultural festivals that celebrated diversity in Korea. The hard part about multicultural education, however, deals with much deeper, critical concepts of difference and discrimination as they are rooted in power relations among the various stakeholders of society. Recognizing the need for a more systematic approach to educating the teachers who can competently lead lessons about diversity in classrooms, the Ministry of Education began to support various research projects and diversity-related curriculum development (Ministry of Education and Human Resources Development, 2006, 2007, & 2008).

---

[14]The law consisted of four principal aims: adopt rational immigration policies, promote social integration of foreigners, define and establish immigration administration, and enhance and support foreigner rights. The main body that emerged from this law is the Immigration Policy Commission, which consisted of a diverse array of constituents from both government and non-government entities (Ministry of Justice, 2012, p. 12).

Chapter 2

Labor Unions, Civil Society, and Immigrant Labor: The Exceptional Case of South Korea

The remarkable solidarity of Korea's civil society organizations (CSOs) and their unwavering advocacy of international migrants stand out because of the positive outcomes and, perhaps more importantly, the way they minimized xenophobic movement. These endeavors yielded a significant modification of the nationality law, expanded the labor and human rights of immigrant workers, and set the stage for the Korean society to embrace social and cultural changes toward multiculturalism. Conversely, anti-immigrant rhetoric or movement in Korea has yet to take root, precisely because the diversity of organizations advocating for the rights of migrants and multicultural families simultaneously weakened the rhetorical power of such ideologies, preempted the possibility of forging a critical mass of anti-immigrant organizations, and kindled agreeable relations with the host society. Perhaps, too, one could count toward its success the organizational strength of non-government organizations, the political opportunity structure, and a myriad of mechanisms that supported the discursive framing and embedding of *damunhwa* (literally multiculture in Korean) in all segments of the Korean society. A striking facet of Korea's effort to integrate immigrants was the role of its progressive labor union, the Korean Confederation of Trade Unions (KCTU), in aligning politically with immigrant advocacy organizations since its inception in 1995. This is important since there are numerous examples worldwide that demonstrate the deleterious effects and regressive stances of labor unions on the question of immigration.

The unique articulation of labor unions' support of immigrant rights and their demonstration of resolute solidarity with migrant workers truly separate the Korean case from the experiences of other labor-receiving countries. The context for this outcome is rooted in Korea's labor movement history that developed out of the rapid industrialization period from the 1960s to the 1980s when the successive military dictators unabashedly supported major conglomerates.

Organized Labor and Civil Society for Multiculturalism: A Solidarity Success Story from South Korea, 25–44

doi:10.1108/978-1-83982-388-620200002

A rally held on an evening in November 2017 captures the historical relevance of Korea's labor movement in contemporary society. In commemorating the 30th and 47th anniversaries of the Great Workers' Struggle[1] and the passing of a labor martyr, Jeon Tae-il, respectively, the KCTU workers filled the streets of Sejong-daero.[2] They were flanked by the Korea Alliance for Progressive Movement[3] (or *jinboyondae* in Korean), the Korean Construction Workers' Union, the Korean Metal Workers' Union, the Korean Teachers and Education Workers' Union, the various KCTU subsidiaries, the Part-Time Workers' Union, and the Migrant Trade Union (MTU). Their main slogan was simple and direct: Secure the right of all laborers to form unions. This was indeed a remarkable statement in that it implicitly referenced the 2015 landmark decision of the Supreme Court of Korea regarding the legal definition of a laborer and appealed the rightful protection of all such workers under Korea's Labor Standards Act. The legal case involved unauthorized migrant workers who had demanded their right to form labor unions, and the Supreme Court ruled in favor of the workers, stipulating that "anyone who provided their labor in exchange for a wage was considered a laborer." Historically, the person who came to symbolize the long and difficult struggle of laborers in Korea was a 22-year-old young man named Jeon Tae-il who, on November 13, 1970, defiantly and publicly protested the dreadful working conditions of seamstresses by immolating himself as his final words echoed across Seoul's Pyonghwa (Peace) Market, "We are not machines – We are human beings – Give us a day of rest – Observe the Labor Standards Act!" The November 2017 demonstration powerfully conjoined these two historic events: the first one awakening the sensibilities of ordinary workers to resist against the inhumane employer abuse and sparking waves of nationwide labor protests, while the latter widening the legal definition of laborer that now transcends the borders of nationality and legal resident status.[4]

---

[1]The Great Workers' Struggle refers to massive cases of labor "stoppages, wildcat strikes, or demonstrations," totaling over three-thousand incidents during the period between July to September 1987 (Koo, 2002, p. 157).

[2]"Sejong" refers to the name of the Korean king who, among other things, is known for inventing and popularizing the Korean alphabet, making written communication much more accessible to common people. "Dero" literally means "big street," and thus, it would be equivalent to an avenue or boulevard. Sejongdero both symbolically and physically represents the heart of public gathering place for all types of political persuasions. It lies directly south of the Blue House, and thus, the President can have a clear view of the goings on in the city center.

[3]Established on September 16, 2007, this umbrella organization focused on four major social issues, including the resistance against the Korea–US Free Trade Agreement, the elimination of contingency employee system that favored employers, the peaceful negotiations between the Koreas and the withdrawal of American troops from the Korean peninsula, and the repeal of the National Security Law.

[4]At the center of such a symbolic moment was a long-time labor advocate named Park Seok-Woon who played a critical role in bridging ties between the progressive national trade union and migrant workers.

Politics of Culture, Anti-immigration, and Labor Unions: A Global Context

In many countries of immigration, trade unions have historically guarded their economic and social position against the perceived immigrant threat. In Australia and Canada, for instance, the labor market segmentation in the contemporary period reflects an institutional continuity where ethnic differences and discrimination within labor movement presented significant challenges for social cohesion and economic equity (Lacovetta, Quinlan, & Radforth, 1996). Wiggen (2012) observed that the Labor Party in Norway during the 2005 Labor Day celebration had committed to solving the immigration problem against which "ordinary people" ought to be protected. This was not surprising given that the trade unions and the political Left framed immigration as a national problem on their political agenda during the 1970s. In the United States, a right-wing political strategist sought to capitalize on anti-immigration constituents within the Democratic Party, including African Americans, unionists, and environmentalists, by claiming that "Republicans ought to welcome them" (Diamond, 1996). Concerned about the recent influx of immigrants, Polish trade unions entertained the possibility of establishing cross-border solidarity with sender countries in order to prevent social dumping, wage decline, and working condition deterioration (Hardy & Fitzgerald, 2010). In welfare states like Sweden, immigration always has been a sensitive topic where organized labor typically opposes "open immigration policies and the ready access of foreigners to social benefits" (Johansson, 2014). Thus, since the 1960s, the Swedish Trade Union Confederation quite practically exercised "welfare chauvinism" in order to regulate labor supply, control access to permanent residency, and minimize the overall effects on the welfare state services (Johansson, 2014).

While trade unions' formal position on immigration issues can potentially impact border policies, anti-immigrant antagonisms and sentiments continue to shape social relations and cultural integration long after the policy debate ends. Irrespective of the truth, these perceptions begin to resonate with the broader population when cultural and institutional mechanisms consistently reinvigorate these claims in highly publicized venues, such as mass media, political speeches, anti-immigrant organizations, and national laws. The politicization of immigration issues globally is clearly on the rise as people have been moving across borders in unprecedented numbers for a wide array of reasons. Populist ideologies prey on common people's fear about perceived international competition (Rooduijn, 2015), but economic factors alone do not account for the spread of xenophobia. In the Netherlands, Awad (2012, p. 169) argues, "anxiety about ethnic minorities" prompted a major change in Dutch policy from multiculturalism to a policy of integration. This retreat from multicultural policy reveals two sides of cultural politics: the perspective relies on "simplistic and static images of what minority identities are" on the one hand and "assumes an authentic national identity, based on a common culture and history" on the other hand (Awad, 2012, p. 170). Shapiro (1997, p. 2) stretches this analysis a bit further by stating that immigrants "constitute an ontological disturbance in the stories people seek to appropriate" and, as such, "disrupt national stories." "Today's immigration alarmists," he points out, "argue on cultural rather than race or biological grounds" (p. 3).

The politics of perception about immigration can progress from discursive frames that feed on populist fear to formalized political parties whose platform articulates policy measures regarding immigration and immigrants.[5] The Centrum Partij in the Netherlands represents one of the first countries to achieve parliamentary representation in Western Europe based on its anti-immigration stance (Van Heerden De Lange, Van der Brug, & Fennema, 2014). Beginning in the 1990s, the Finns Party in Finland has gained significant popular support on anti-immigration platform. Despite their visible references to the lyrics of the *Socialist Internacionale*, the Progress Party of Norway has been quite intentional about excluding international workers from joining trade unions and pitting the interests of "ordinary people" against immigrants (Wiggen, 2012). According to Rooduijn (2015, p. 3), the rise of populist radical right parties in Western Europe reflects not only the onset of globalization across these liberal democracies but also specific social and political developments that support political parties with increasingly "nativist, populist and Eurosceptic positions." Not all scholars agree on the notion that there is in fact a "rising tide of anti-immigration" in Europe, but instead the formation of anti-immigration parties may be attributed to an activation of "a shrinking segment" of western European populations whose "preexisting dispositions against immigration" became more prevalent and salient. "Some aspects of immigration," Dennison and Geddes (2019, p. 108) argue, "that are most deemed to threaten conservative values like security, tradition or conformity have activated already existing anti-immigration sentiment."

From Italy to Poland, the anti-immigrant sentiment in Europe is on the rise, however. The increasing visibility of immigrants and refugees from nation-states that are perceived to clash with the culture of host societies greatly increases the presence of antiforeigner sentiments. According to United Kingdom's *The Independent* newspaper, Italy leads the top five anti-immigrant countries in Europe, followed by France, Germany, Spain, and United Kingdom.[6] While it is not a comprehensive measure of the "anti-immigrant" level, a significant number of respondents affirmed the statement, "there are so many foreigners living here, it doesn't feel like home anymore." As of January 2018, some 4.34 million foreign-born population who came from non-European Union (EU) member states resided in Italy, accounting for 7.2% of the total population. In France, the

---

[5]Portice and Reicher (2018) argue that anti-immigrant antagonisms do not ordinarily develop from people's cognitions but are generally mobilized by political actors. High-profile anti-immigration mobilization by prominent political leaders generates antipathy as a way of defending the interests of a larger group. The authors observe that doing so allows them to achieve political authority that may help them get elected in countries like the United Kingdom.

[6]See the article, "The Most Anti-Immigrant Countries in Europe." Retrieved from https://www.independent.co.uk/news/world/europe/europe-immigration-most-anti-immigrant-countries-italy-france-germany-uk-a7460301.html.

number was significantly higher (6.04 million or 9%), while Germany recorded the highest number (7.79 million or 9.4 %), and Spain and the United Kingdom also showed a significant proportion of foreign-born population at 4.27 million (9.2%) and 5.74 million (8.7%), respectively.[7] Incidentally, the top five anti-immigrant countries demonstrated a relatively lower level of union density, ranging from the lowest of 8% of the total employees currently in French unions to 35% in Italy. The figures for the highest union density was led by Finland (74%), followed by Sweden (70%), Denmark (67%), Norway (52%), and Belgium (50%). While it is difficult to draw a direct association between anti-immigrant sentiments and key indicators such as the proportion of foreign-born population or union density, it appears that countries with a higher level of foreign-born from non-EU member states expressed a higher level of dissatisfaction with the presence of foreigners and simultaneously demonstrated lower levels of union density. Such preliminary findings may suggest that labor unions could play a much more assertive role in mediating the politics of culture with regard to immigration and social integration of immigrant populations (Table 2.1).

In the United States, anti-immigrant organizations, political parties, and labor unions significantly influenced the parameters of immigration policies historically. Each of these constituents had different motives for opposing immigration from extreme xenophobia and political opportunism to cultural and social protectionism. These fault lines developed and widened based on the perceived and real differences of cultures, languages, and mores. But, the society's elites, including the scientists, academics, and ministers, not only contributed to ethnic conflicts but also socially embedded the idea that races are inherently – that is, from their birth – different from one another, thus hopeless to try to change through cultural acquisition. Within such cultural contexts, labor unions too capitalized on the extant stereotypes about particular ethnic populations in order to galvanize support for their exclusion. The US history is replete with examples where, particularly during the downswing of economic cycles, exclusionary movements intensified. For decades in the last century, democrats had been concerned about the contradictory interests among the constituents, namely, the ethnic immigrant minorities and labor unions, because of the latter group's historical opposition to immigration generally and undocumented immigrants specifically. This position, however, changed abruptly in 2000 when the American Federation of Labor and Congress of Industrial Organizations (AFL-CIO) offered support for developing pathways to citizenship for undocumented immigrants.[8]

[7]These figures retrieved from Eurostat, "Statistics Explained." Retrieved from https://ec.europa.eu/eurostat/statistics-explained/pdfscache/1275.pdf. Accessed on October 7, 2019. The foreign-born share of the total population in these five countries averaged about 8.7%.

[8]See the article, "How the Labor Movement Did a 180 on Immigration." Retrieved from https://www.npr.org/2013/02/05/171175054/how-the-labor-movement-did-a-180-on-immigration. Accessed on October 7, 2019. Since the changes in their official position, labor unions have fought against deportation of unauthorized immigrants, backed

Table 2.1. Migrant Populations and Union Density in Select European Union Countries.

	Foreign Born (Within European Union)		Foreign Born (Outside European Union)		Union Density, % of Employee	Anti-immigrant, Question (% Yes)
	Thousand	**% Pop.**	**Thousand**	**% Pop.**		
Italy	1,832	3.0	4,342	7.2	35	52
France	2,142	3.2	6,035	9.0	8	47
Germany	5,951	7.2	7,794	9.4	18	44
Spain	1,925	4.1	4,273	9.2	19	38
United Kingdom	3,768	5.7	5,743	8.7	26	37
Finland	124	2.3	239	4.3	74	30
Sweden	550	5.4	1,325	13.1	70	33
Denmark	238	4.1	452	7.8	67	25
Norway	353	6.7	468	8.8	52	NA
Belgium	886	7.8	1,029	9.0	50	NA

Source: Migrant population statistics (as of January 1, 2018) drawn from Eurostat, https://ec.europa.eu/eurostat/statistics-explained/pdfscache/1275.pdf; the union density figures (various years between 2008 and 2014) compiled from "worker-participation.eu," https://www.worker-participation.eu/National-Industrial-Relations/Across-Europe/Trade-Unions2; the data for the anti-immigrant EU country reflect the percent agreeing with the statement, "there are so many foreigners living here, it doesn't feel like home anymore," https://www.independent.co.uk/news/world/europe/europe-immigration-most-anti-immigrant-countries-italy-france-germany-uk-a7460301.html. Accessed on October 7, 2019.

In the context of declining union membership nationally, America's largest union made a practical decision to change their position regarding the presumed impact of particularly less-skilled immigrants on the labor market. Consequently, the fastest growing unions in the post-2000 period consist of service unions, such as Service Employees International Union (SEIU), where many of their new members have been recent immigrants, both authorized and unauthorized.

immigration reforms, and supported providing tuition and financial aid benefits to dreamers. The following articles provide background information: https://newrepublic.com/article/113203/labor-and-immigration-how-unions-got-board-immigration-reform; https://www.huffpostbrasil.com/entry/organized-labor-steps-up-to-fight-deportations_n_59b6df97e4b03e6197afea7c; https://www.usw.org/blog/2019/workers-of-the-world-unite-at-last Accessed on October 7, 2019.

Korean Confederation of Trade Unions

Korea's trade unions developed and transformed in response to the changes in political and economic landscapes. During the formative decade following the end of the Korean War in 1953, the Federation of Korean Trade Unions (*Hankooknochong*) (FKTU) formed under the tutelage of the US-backed President Rhee Syngman who was concerned about the communist ideology spreading within the labor ranks. Immediately after the failed civil uprising on April 19, 1960, an army general, Park Chung-hee, led a military coup d'etat the following year and successive, authoritarian regimes followed until the first democratic election of 1987. During this period, the military leadership focused on rapid economic development and fostered the creation of conglomerates or *chaebol* enterprises, while severely suppressing all opposition from civilian and labor groups. They often resorted to state violence and military-run cultural-reform schools to which protesters had been sent for an intense disciplinary re-education program. Despite harsh repression by the authoritarian government, the working-class Koreans maintained the spirit of resistance fueled by the widespread support from *minjung*, a broad swath of newly formed middle class, who vocalized their critical view of the government by participating in street protests, organizing factory workers, and forming labor unions. The pressure for societal change had been building for several decades until in 1987 when the first democratically elected President Roh Tae-Woo, who was ironically an underling of Park Chung-hee in the military, began to show signs of loosening state control through tolerating opposition voices, supporting free press, and creating autonomous governing boards in education. The opening of such political opportunity contributed to "the largest labor unrest" in Korea's modern history (Koo, 2002, p. 157). The Great Workers' Struggle lasted for 3 months beginning in July 1987 when over 3,000 cases of labor conflicts destabilized the very foundation of Korea's cultural and economic structure and led to the formation of the Korea Trade Union Congress (KTUC or *cheonnohyup* in Korean) in January 1990 (J. Kim, 2003).

Emerging from the massive energy of people yearning for democratic freedom and labor liberation, KTUC provided an alternative platform on which to build a more radical, militant ideology. In addition to the blue-collar worker base, the white-collar trade unions created the Korea Congress of Independent Industrial Trade Union Federations, which combined forces with KTUC and formed the Korean Council of Trade Union Representatives (H. Song, 1999). Several years later, on the 25th anniversary of the passing of Jeon Tae-il, the new groups morphed into the KCTU, which stood on the cusp of social change as it struggled to make fundamental labor and social reforms. In its founding declaration, the KCTU members recalled the painful history of their predecessors who fought for the national liberation, resisted against authoritarian regimes, and now they vowed to establish a national organization of workers based on the principles of autonomy and democracy. "In fulfilling our mission of securing basic human rights and dignity," they proclaimed, "we shall strive to achieve basic labor rights, eliminate undemocratic labor practices, and bring forces to bear on the struggle to eradicate industrial accidents and to actualize gender equality." Their cause was not simply a labor issue, but it was entwined with democratic reforms through which they sought to improve everyone's quality of life, coupled with a goal of achieving the country's sovereignty, democracy, and unification through persistent struggle. As well, they pledged to establish solidarity with workers of the world and to bring about world peace through elimination of wars and nuclear weapons. "Let us not," they declared, "succumb to the trickeries of capitalists or buckle before the repressive power but raise our union flags proudly and march forward until our fight for one democratic Korea is finally won!" (KCTU). The newly formed KCTU was perhaps overly ambitious in its outlook and grandiose in rhetoric, but in practice, their commitment to support international migrant workers was both historic and forward-looking despite some differing opinions among the rank-and-file workers.[9]

The emergence of KCTU in November 1995 coincided with the consolidation of CSOs seeking to take up the international migrant worker concerns.[10] Many of these religious and citizen groups had worked together previously on a range of social and labor issues; the CSO leaders emerged in the context of raging protests against the repressive government of the previous decades. They knew how to organize and protest, and they were unafraid to speak their minds about the need to fight for the society's vulnerable populations and to make the government and responsible parties accountable for creating conditions of inequality. Despite their many years of organizing experience, the CSO leaders quite naturally viewed the international worker issue from diverse perspectives. Initially, however, the various cases of glaring workplace abuse against the foreign industrial trainees became the most pressing issue at the time. Just a few years into the start of the trainee system, 11 trainees-turned-unauthorized workers from Nepal and Bangladesh waged the first migrant worker protest at the Citizens' Coalition for Economic Justice (CCEJ) building in January 1994, demanding the Korean government to compensate the injured workers and to bring justice to employers who treated them inhumanely. This first public outcry drew national attention in several important ways: first, the fact that Korea started to receive international workers was historic; second, although they entered as temporary guest workers, many overstayed their visas or left the factories and became unauthorized workers; third, employers and Korean co-workers often abused migrant workers who came from poorer countries and looked visibly different. From the vantage point of CSOs, the migrant workers represented a significant challenge since they were unfamiliar with non-Koreans who spoke different languages and practiced foreign religions and customs. Perhaps the most expedient and sensible approach at the time was exactly the path that they took: secure their basic human dignity and labor rights. The migrant workers' legal status as trainees and unauthorized workers became the focus of their advocacy, not their cultural diversity or the prospect of their long-term settlement in Korea. No one could have predicted then that some 25 years hence Korea would evolve into a multicultural society.

---

[9]Prior to the official launching of the Industrial Trainee System, the Labor Minister announced a plan in 1991 to bring in migrant workers in the city of Taebaek but was met with a stiff opposition from FKTU (Cho, 2001).

[10]For a comprehensive history, see K. Park (2002).

Even before its official launch, KCTU demonstrated institutional support for migrant worker struggle at CCEJ demonstration in 1994, albeit only declaratively and symbolically. The following year, when the 13 Nepalese workers waged another protest at Myung-dong Catholic Cathedral, KCTU showed their support and solidarity, together with numerous alliance organizations.[11] As the stories about the migrant worker plight intensified, civil society leaders representing citizen groups, labor, and religious organizations established a Joint Taskforce Committee (*gongdaewi*) of which a KCTU preparation-committee member was a part. At the international seminar in Seoul, sponsored by the Friedrich-Ebert-Stiftung Foundation, in May 1995, a KCTU representative read the union's official position statement on migrant labor that captured an internationalist perspective regarding labor and capital. It read:

> What are the structural reasons for the constant growth of migrant population throughout the world? On the surface, it is explained by wage differences arising from economic disparities between the Third World and the advanced countries. But, such an argument ignores the fact that the advanced countries' "development of underdevelopment" policies massively produce industrial reserve army of labor, subordinate labor to transnational corporations, and exploit the surplus generated in the process... Consequently, the pattern of international labor migration is a direct result of the international movement of capital, including our country's capital. These transnational corporations' direct investments in manufacturing disrupted their agricultural and traditional mode of life and created today's industrial proletariat, who is being forced out of their country in search of jobs. For these reasons, the advanced countries and the transnational corporations are both suppliers and consumers of foreign workers. Correspondingly foreign workers represent our creditors and guests.[12]

---

[11]These organizations include Citizens' Coalition for Economic Justice, Federation of Korean YMCA, Practicing Christian Ethics Movement, Eastern Learning National Unification Association, Federation of Judo Associations, and Won Buddhism, International Citizen Volunteer Association, Korean Evergreen Society, Association for Citizens' New Consciousness Movement, Institute for Regional Parliamentary Government, Young Christian Physicians' Association, Young Doctors of Eastern Medicine Association, Federation of Korean Women Voters, Research Center for Korean Women in Politics, Women's Association for Korean Unification, Federation of Korean Trade Unions, Association of the National Trade Union Representatives, Association of Korean Women Workers, San-dol Labor Cultural Center, Labor Rights Organization, Korean Episcopal Church, Korean Presbyterian Church, Association for Foreign Worker Mission, Association of Buddhists Supporting National Unification, Association of Korean Buddhist Professors, Foreign Worker Shelter, Foreign Worker Association, and Kuro Jubilee Mission Church.

[12]Quoted in Kim (2003, pp. 255–256). Original, in Korean, translated by the author from W. Yoon (1995).

The groundswell of support from the cross-section of Korea's civil society eventually led to the formation of an umbrella group called the Joint Committee for Migrant Workers in Korea (JCMK)[13] in the summer of 1995, and the Committee immediately planned an involvement of some 39 CSO groups in sponsoring three major public events.[14] That November, another chapter in Korea's labor history would be made by officially launching KCTU with the help of some 866 trade unions and 410,000 union members.[15]

In the first 10 years of KCTU's existence, its role in taking up migrant worker issues would undergo significant transformation. The complex circumstances shaped the trajectory of the relationship among the key stakeholders, including KCTU, JCMK, and migrant worker organizations. As a newly formed national trade union, KCTU contended with its own precarious legal status since its official recognition by the Korean government did not occur until 2002, while they were struggling to force a release of their new labor leader, Kwon Young-Gil, who had been arrested for violating a labor law.[16] More importantly, a number of practical questions about how to organize migrant workers naturally emerged, including principally the legality of organizing contracted trainees and unauthorized workers (KCTU, 2002a). The percentage of unauthorized workers vis-à-vis other migrant workers ranged from the low of 58.9% by the end of 1994 to its peak at 78.4% in 2003 (J. Kim, 2003, p. 246). Clearly, the trainee system had systematically generated unauthorized workers, but it was not clear whether such workers would be able to join a labor union.[17] Based on KCTU's survey on union workers' attitude on various key topics, some 37.8% of those surveyed expressed that "it would be more desirable to not employ migrant workers because it can be a hindrance to hiring domestic workers," even though 43.9% also said that "foreign workers should be given the same rights to join a labor union and to be treated equally as domestic workers" (KCTU, 2000). The diversity of alliance groups within JCMK also presented a significant challenge in that the major fault line developed around two broad, ideological differences about the nature of the problem and the solution to follow. That is, there were some groups that focused

[13]Later, the name changed to Joint Committee *with* Migrant Workers in Korea in recognition of its paternalistic bias in the original name that used the preposition "for."

[14]The three events included: first, on October 25, they held a press conference regarding the position paper titled "our opinions on ways to resolve migrant worker issues," which was signed by some 650 CSO leaders; second, in the afternoon on the same day, they sponsored a public hearing to amend the Foreign Worker Protection Law; and, finally, on October 29, they celebrated migrant worker cultural diversity at Yonsei University where over 2,000 migrant workers participated. For more discussion, see S. Park (1996).

[15]KCTU. Retrieved from http://nodong.org/history. Accessed on October 16, 2019.

[16]In 1996, the majority New Korea Party forced a new labor law by holding an emergency meeting in the middle of the night. The amended law made firing workers much easier and prohibited representation of national unions at local and national levels, which delegitimized KCTU but prompted massive strikes.

[17]The battle to determine whether unauthorized workers would be legally eligible to join a labor union would be fought in the courts.

on advocating on behalf of migrant workers as they have been under JCMK, and thus, the bulk of their work centered on providing legal and labor counseling services. At the same time, organizations that viewed migrant workers from a critical labor perspective articulated different approaches, with a focus on overcoming labor precarity of migrants and building capacity for their own advocacy.

Despite its internal and external complexities, KCTU never relented on its demonstration of support for migrant workers' rights. In collaboration with JCMK, KCTU leadership protested against the flawed trainee system and participated in public demonstrations in support of the passage of the Foreign Worker Protection Law. Table 2.2 further shows KCTU continuously aligned with JCMK and other progressive CSOs both domestically and internationally in helping to broaden the boundaries of civil and labor rights of migrant workers (J. Kim, 2005). Aside from these highly visible demonstrations, KCTU members continuously engaged in public conversations through forums and hearings held in their own very office buildings in order to advance its position and to aid the CSOs in achieving fair treatment of migrant workers. For some, such activities did not meet their expectations. They would have wanted KCTU to take a much more assertive role in organizing migrant workers by bringing them into the ranks of other Korean unionists and educating Korean workers about the global economic system that causes international migration. More importantly, they recognized that KCTU was uniquely positioned to support the development of migrant-worker trade-unions in due course. These expectations would be partly fulfilled in October 2000, but the deeper struggles of achieving complete labor rights would continue for a few more decades.

Migrant Trade Union (Seoul-Kyunggi-Inchon Area)

Some 30 years after Jeon Tae-il's unforgettable public outcry, migrant workers in Korea are reciting those very same words. "We are not machines – We are human!" "Observe the labor laws." To these, they have added several more slogans: "All Workers are One!" "Stop EPS ... Stop Crackdown," "Free Job Change," "Achieve WPS," "I Am Not Your Slave!" The migrant workers in Korea represent both a continuation of decades-old struggle and a new chapter in its labor movement history.[18] It is indeed remarkably ironic to witness these chants on the streets of Seoul led by people who look visibly at odds with the dominant Korean population. From 1994 to 2000, the number of migrant workers increased fourfold from about 70,000 to 280,000 (J. Kim, 2003, p. 246). All of the workers had entered Korea as industrial trainees, but by the year's end in 2000, some 64% had become unauthorized workers. Moreover, all of the workers who led these protests risked deportation. The story behind the radicalization of migrant labor population starts with the 1994 protest at CCEJ and numerous other subsequent demonstrations. The year 2000, however, marks a new era in migrant worker activism where

[18]For a synopsis of migrant worker movement history, see Chung (2012).

Table 2.2. A Brief History of KCTU Solidarity Projects with Migrant Workers, 1994–2005.

January 1994	11 workers from Nepal and Bangladesh protest at CCEJ regarding industrial accidents, physical abuse, forced labor, violation of human, and labor rights
October 27, 1994	FKTU, a precursor to KCTU, participates in a forum titled "Modern-day slavery: a discussion on improving human rights situation of foreign industrial trainees"
November 25, 1994	KCTU Preparation Committee promotes a campaign to "improve human rights condition of foreign industrial trainees"
January 1995	Supports 13-member Nepalese protest at Myung-dong Catholic Church
July 1995	Participates as a founding organization of JCMK – the office space made available at KCTU; agrees to form labor unions for migrants
November 11, 1995	KCTU established
1996–1997	Supports a petition drive to pass the Foreign Worker Protection Law and participates in a protest at Myongdong to amend a labor law
1998 spring	Support the creation of migrant community leader group, the International Migrants' Organization in Korea (IMOK)
December 18, 1998	Prominent church and CSO leaders, including KCTU directors, participate in "migrant worker international solidarity day"
November 3, 1999	JCMK sponsors a forum titled "The Prospect of Foreign Worker Movement and Labor Union Formation"; KCTU Policy Director Yoon, Wu-Hyun presents on solidarity between migrant and Korean workers
October 2000	Supports the creation of Migrant Worker Headquarter for Achieving Complete Labor Rights and Actualizing Freedom of Movement and Employment (MWSH)
May 2001	Seoul-Kyungin-Area Equality Trade Union – Migrant Worker Division (ETU-MWD) established
2002	KCTU's Construction Trade Union estimates some 22,000 to 25,000 migrant workers of 1.76 million workers in the construction industry
April 7, 2002	About 1,000 migrant workers gathered at Dongdaemun Training Park and decided to "refuse registration of unauthorized migrant workers and to achieve legalization"
May 9, 2002	Supports the creation of "a joint taskforce to eliminate migrant worker repression and to achieve work visas" – grant the right of legal residence and employment

Table 2.2. *(Continued)*

June 16, 2002	Supports MWSH demonstration at Jongmyo Park – Bangladesh worker shouts "Workers of the World are One!" in his native language
September 2002 to November 2002	In anticipation of the passage of a new labor importation plan, the government raids factories and deports about 920 unauthorized workers
October 2002	Korean irregular workers and migrants together form Sungsuh Labor Union in Daegu and selects co-leaders with a migrant worker as a vice president
August 2003	EPS passes; deportation of unauthorized workers intensifies
November 2003 to December 2004	Myongdong protest against deportation; departs from citizen supported human rights protest to independent labor protest; the first KCTU-ETU-MWD protest
April 24, 2005	MTU of Seoul-Kyunggi-Inchon Areas launched; an independent MTU joins KCTU's Seoul Headquarter
2006	Recommends implementation of a quota system to include women, irregular, and migrant workers at a conference of delegates
2006	Migrant workers join the metal workers' union in Daegu's Sahmwu Precision Metal Company
2009	Federation of Korean Metal Workers' Trade Unions publishes a report on the migrant worker working conditions
2009	Kyong-ju region Metal Workers' Trade Union receives migrant workers into its union
September 29, 2010	Bilateral Union Memorandum of Understanding signed between KCTU and Nepalese Trade Union; KCTU issues a compact book titled *Migrant Worker Rights* in seven languages
2013	Kyong-ju region's M. S. Auto-tech organizes migrant workers into its trade union; an Indonesian worker elected as a metal workers' union officer
2015	The Supreme Court of Korea decides that the MTU is constitutional

Source: The author translated and compiled from KCTU (2014).

their efforts would coalesce much more organically with KCTU and other CSO leaders who prioritize labor over other struggles.

Unlike other countries of immigration, Korea's migrant population represents a small fraction of the entire workforce. The speed with which migrant workers in Korea gained a sense of class-conscious position is remarkable, and it could not have been possible without the support and solidarity of Korean labor leaders. In the first decade of their struggle in Korea, CSOs and JCMK were vitally important in articulating and propagating the human and labor rights abuses, thus gaining wide public sympathy and laying the groundwork for much more directed and organized labor struggle. The first step in this direction occurred in October 2000 when some members of JCMK and migrant worker organization practitioners would join hands to form the Migrant Worker Struggle Headquarter for Achieving Complete Labor Rights and Actualizing Freedom of Movement and Employment (MWSH). The splintering of MWSH from JCMK reflects both the maturation of migrant labor movement and KCTU's rearticulation of migrant labor issues.[19] While one of the goals of MWSH was to achieve autonomy for migrant workers, this could not be possible without the help of the experienced Korean activists who can navigate the complex legal and social systems. Their new demand reflected a significant change in how they began to approach the labor struggle: instead of the "Foreign Worker Protection Law," the migrant workers wanted the same labor rights as domestic workers. That is, at the very minimum, the complete *nodong sahmkwon* (three primary labor rights), which includes the right to organize, the right to collective bargaining, and the right to collective action.

In reflecting back on these formative years of migrant worker activism, an Executive Director of the Migrant Labor Movement Solidarity Committee[20] commented that KCTU had not then fully embraced migrant worker issues as its priority but only demonstrated symbolic support and solidarity (Y. Chung, 2014). A month before the formation of MWSH, JCMK sponsored a forum titled "The Prospect of Foreign Worker Movement and Labor Union Formation," where the KCTU Policy Director, Yoon Wu-Hyun, presented on KCTU's unwavering support of migrant workers and emphasized the need to establish solidarity

---

[19]In his criticism of JCMK, the MWSH Director of Organizational Solidarity (*jo-jikyeondae gukjang*), Cho Dae-hwan (2001) observed that while it initially provided invaluable service to migrant workers through its rights-based advocacy work, the organization ultimately (1) failed to establish as its purpose the effort to target factors that fundamentally contribute to labor exploitation; (2) thus unable to overcome the structural contradictions that produce inequality; and (3) furthermore stunted the ability of migrant workers to stand on their own two feet.

[20]This Committee was formed in response to the increasing government repression of migrant workers upon launching of the Employment Permit System in 2003, which eventually would phase out the Industrial Trainee System. The main purpose of the Committee consisted of three basic aims: (1) to support migrant workers in their struggle to become an autonomous movement; (2) to advocate for legalization of unauthorized workers, abolition of the trainee system, and securing of *nodong sahmkwon* (three basic labor rights) and the right to change workplaces; (3) to administer all matters dealing with fundraising and fund management, distribution of promotion materials, and logistics of sustaining solidarity activities with migrant workers in Korea. Some of the key people who supported the creation of this Committee included prominent KCTU leaders, including Kwon Young-gil (the first term president) and Dahn Byung-ho (president at the time of the Committee formation). Retrieved from http://migrants.jinbo.net/index1.htm. Accessed on October 24, 2019.

with Korean workers by joining its labor union.[21] Furthermore, Director Yoon articulated a long-term strategy that would include organizing migrant workers, together with small company and irregular workers, by establishing a committee or a taskforce with explicit support for its organizing activities. In response, the JCMK Director, Lee Geum-Yeon, vowed to support migrant workers in their effort to take ownership of labor union organizing (Weekly Donga, 2003). Although such exchanges may seem only symbolic for the critics, their consistently affirmative stances in public venues impact future events. For migrant workers in Korea, that critical moment came in May 2001 when the Equality Trade Union-Migrant Worker Division of Seoul-Kyeongin-Inchon-Area was launched (ETU-MWD). Again, the KCTU leadership echoed the familiar sentiments:

> In the past the migrant worker issues had been relegated to the sidelines of KCTU, but from this day forward we earnestly pledge our commitment to work together and to lighten the burden from their shoulders. (Y. Lee, 2014, p. 25)

Buoyed by support from KCTU, migrant workers initiated several highly visible public protests. By the end of 2001, the Ministry of Justice recorded a total of 333,000 migrant workers, of whom some 77.4% had turned into unauthorized workers. Because of such a structural flaw in the trainee system, the migrant workers naturally sought to address their legal precarity. On April 7, 2002, about 1,000 migrant workers gathered at Dongdaemun Training Facility Park and decided to protest against the government's mandate that unauthorized workers register their places of work and residence. They also demanded the government to legalize all unauthorized workers. In the following two months, the momentum gained greater force as they created a Joint Taskforce that would focus on resisting against government's repression, advocating for adoption of the work visa program, and securing the legal right of residence and work for migrants. In carrying out these tasks at a protest rally, a Bangladesh worker shouted the following words in his native language: "All workers of the world are one!"[22] These sentiments were echoed repeatedly in a migration conference held at the central KCTU building in Seoul, which was sponsored by ETU-MWD, on February 23, 2003.[23] The migrant workers in Korea were becoming increasingly radicalized,

---

[21]Retrieved from http://www.newscham.net/news/view.php?board=news&id=9474. Accessed on October 24, 2019.

[22]The demonstration was held on June 16, 2002, at Jongmyo Square Park.

[23]Prior to this conference, KCTU made its position clear in other venues. At a "Legislative Public Hearing on Foreign Worker Employment and Securing Basic Rights" (KCTU, 2002b), held at the National Assembly, a KCTU representative presented its official position. It consisted of the following key terms: (1), implement a work permit system that is consistent with and in recognition of migrant workers' legitimate status as laborers; (2) providing migrant workers with the right to change their workplaces can prevent human rights violations and labor exploitation; (3) extend the

and it became clearer that they did not yet have the capacity to wage a protracted struggle without the Korean supporters.

In August 2003, the National Assembly finally passed a new law that would eventually phase out the controversial Industrial Trainee System. The new law titled "Foreign Worker Employment and Related Law,"[24] which activated the Employment Permit System (EPS), was intended to address the main problems of the trainee system, including the recruitment of trainees by a for-profit organization, the preponderance of trainees-turned-unauthorized workers, and the stabilization of domestic labor market through a careful control and management of migrant worker population (J. Kim, 2005). Unlike some of the progressive citizens groups, like JCMK, that grudgingly supported EPS, the newly formed ETU-MWD forcefully resisted against its implementation, principally because the EPS workers could not freely change workplaces and the employers still held unbridled power to renew their contracts.[25] After a series of public protests, the ETU-MWD members and the Nepalese community group waged perhaps the longest migrant labor protest to date, which lasted from November 15, 2003 to November 28, 2004, at the famous Myungdong Catholic Cathedral. For nearly 380 days, they fought back against the government's draconian deportation measures, particularly the targeted crackdown and deportation of ETU-MWD leaders, and demanded complete legalization of all unauthorized workers, the right of all EPS workers to change jobs, and the application of Labor Standards Law to all migrant workers. In other words, they demanded to be treated like any other worker, regardless of ethnicity and legal status (Ko, 2019).

As the battles waged on for months on end, KCTU co-participated substantively in the struggle with migrant workers. Initially, the name of the protest group at Myungdong Catholic Cathedral officially changed to "KCTU Sit-in Protest Group," and the Group was co-represented by the leader of migrants and a vice president of KCTU. Moreover, a new personnel position was created within the central KCTU office in order to exclusively oversee migrant worker issues. Shortly thereafter, on April 24, 2005, an independent MTU formed under

---

term of work permit to five years and renewable every five years, to prevent workers overstaying their visas and becoming unauthorized; and (4), in accordance with the United Nation's various human rights instruments, migrant workers' basic rights should be protected, including the rights to form labor unions, to equal treatment and to equal pay for equal work. Retrieved from http://www.pssp.org/bbs/view.php?board=journal&nid=1113. Accessed on October 24, 2019.

[24]The original version of law can be found here: http://www.law.go.kr/법령/외국인근로자의고용등에관한법률/(06967,20030816). The subsequent amendments can be accessed here: http://www.law.go.kr/법령/외국인근로자의고용등에관한법률.

[25]Lee, Yoon-ju, a former director of ETU-MWD, commented: "At the time when the EPS bill was being discussed at the National Assembly, our members were holding placards opposing its implementation while JCMK brought out a contradicting sign and, in a commanding tone, an executive member told migrants to take down the sign" (KCTU, 2014, p. 22).

the direct jurisdiction of the Seoul Area KCTU Headquarter. The MTU's founding statement declared:

> We are migrant workers who toil daily in Korea .... Our facial pigments, language and religion may be different, but we are laborers just like Koreans who sell their bodies to employers and produce goods for the rest of the world .... We further declare that we intend to achieve our rights as laborers regardless of resident status, thus our right to establish a labor union is unquestionable and justified .... We expect the government will continue to suppress migrant worker rights as they have done before, but we, who have declared our rights now, are determined to organize even greater number of migrant workers and stand shoulder-to-shoulder with Korean workers in solidarity. Lastly, we resolve to march forward until the labor rights of migrants are secured, and, furthermore, until all forms of discrimination, repression and exploitation cease to exist.[26]

The launching of MTU represented another important chapter in Korea's labor movement history, but the government was not quite ready to concede to the demands of migrant workers. In early June, the Ministry of Labor denied MTU's application for the union establishment based on the argument that unauthorized migrant workers are not covered under Korea's three basic labor rights. The legal battle would continue to a High Court where it was decided in February 2007 that unauthorized migrant workers by definition should be considered workers, with full rights and privileges, including the right to join and form a labor union. The Ministry of Labor appealed this decision, and it would take another eight years before the Supreme Court would render its final decision. On June 25, 2015, the Court sided with the workers, stipulating "according to the labor union law, a worker is defined as anyone who works for wages and salaries." Furthermore, the Court declared that "the issue of employability does not preclude the possibility of inclusion within the meaning of the word laborer."[27] In recognition of their long-fought struggle and invaluable contribution to the labor movement, MTU received the Jeon Tae-il Labor Award in 2018. At the commemorative ceremony, the MTU leader, Udaya Lai, proclaimed

> I am thrilled to receive this award today on behalf of one-thousand MTU members and one-million migrant workers in Korea. I vow to fight, as we have done thus far, until all workers are united. Workers of the world, unite![28]

---

[26]Translated from http://migrant.nodong.net/index.php?mid=about. Accessed on October 24, 2019.

[27]Translated from https://wspaper.org/article/15997. Accessed on October 24, 2019.

[28]Translated from http://worknworld.kctu.org/news/articleView.html?idxno=248590. Accessed on October 24, 2019.

Significance of CSOs and Trade Unions in Korean Context

Movement of workers and families across national borders presents challenges for both migrants and host societies. Whether for economic, political, or cultural reasons, the migrants move in order to improve their conditions by taking advantage of opportunities that they perceive exists in another country. Some host societies structurally depend on international workers because of the labor shortage across industries, struggle to develop immigration policies consistent with their liberal democratic ideals, or simply cannot control the cross-border influx of people who may be unwanted culturally. Regardless of the motivations and reasons, migrant populations become subject of intense national debates that both reflect and affirm national identities of the dominant population. The varied expressions of emotions and rationality in public discourses embody implicit desires of who they are as people, what kinds of society they wish to create, and how immigration can serve as a proxy for difference for political gain. Politicians, CSOs, interest groups, and news media all play very significant roles in framing immigration issues, but historically labor unions have played perhaps a decisive role in mediating the politics of immigration. The labor union members generally come from working-class families who perhaps think they have most to lose by competing against immigrant workers. Thus, they are most sensitive to population shifts and how new immigrants become integrated into their workplaces, communities, and societies. The official positions of labor unions on immigrant populations across the globe have changed significantly, and there is little doubt as to how their solidarity with immigrant workers can serve to moderate the spread of xenophobia.

In this regard, Korea's trade unions stand out for several important historical and organizational reasons. First, the cross-movement coalitions between CSOs and trade unions (B. Lee, 2015) developed at a time when migrants began entering Korea. The establishment of JCMK in 1995 and its development of affinity relations across a spectrum of CSOs mutually reinforced progressive values regarding society's vulnerable populations. Because of the organizational diversity, clear differences existed about the specifics of the policy suggestions. However, from a broad historical lens, the manner in which they all embraced migrants in Korea is quite exemplary. While religious leaders, particularly Protestant ministers, assumed leadership roles within JCMK, the integral and critical involvement of longtime labor advocates, such as Park Seok-Woon, complicated the content of advocacy work. The eventual splintering within JCMK based on ideological differences (e.g., mission outreach, human rights observance, worker organizing) was perhaps bound to occur, but what is important to note is that each group perceived migrant workers as a benefit in advancing their respective causes. Unlike the development in some parts of Europe and the Americas, these critical CSOs did not pit economic or cultural interests of the nation against the migrant populations. Thus, in light of its brief history, the consolidation of CSOs and labor unions focused on migrant worker issues in Korea grew exponentially in the most desirable way possible. Their unwavering advocacy for and activism with migrant workers curtailed the spread of xenophobic attitudes that could have easily swept across the Korean society. As a country that prided itself on the myth of homogeneity, Korea certainly had the potential to exhibit the worst forms of discriminatory behaviors, cultural chauvinism, and explicitly racist treatment toward non-Korean, non-Western populations. The fact that xenophobia has not gained substantial traction in Korea can be attributed to the role of CSOs. Trade unions' evolutionary attitude toward migrant workers from the passive-support position to full support of advancing migrant worker rights certainly contributed to the positive environment for their social integration into the Korean society.

Second, the precarious political status of migrant workers presented a significant challenge for labor organizing. A majority of migrant workers were either on short-term (two years) contracts or unauthorized. This situation has not improved significantly even under EPS, since workers are still under three-year contracts. The difference, however, was that, during the formative years, migrant workers were being introduced to the Korean society for the first time. Some of the critics of KCTU have argued that the trade unions could have proactively organized migrant workers earlier rather than merely demonstrating declarative solidarity. Both the timing factor and the symbolic significance of their support cannot be dismissed, however. Timing wise, the Korean society, as much as their fellow Korean laborers, benefited from broad citizens' education about living and working with people from diverse cultures. This was done primarily through advocacy work of citizens and religious organizations who helped to humanize migrant populations by sharing stories of egregious human rights violations. Such stories were quickly soaked up by the news media and developed into talk shows, special programs, and movies. Soon, all sectors of the Korean society, from churches and temples to universities and elementary schools, propagated the images about migrant populations as victims of exploitation and abuse that produced some unintended consequences. Such a deficit model has its own, long-term negative effects, but perhaps it may have been an important way to bring awareness to the pressing social issues at the time. Labor activists certainly could have attempted to educate their Korean workers, promoted broad messages about how migrants fit within the global economic system to the rest of the Korean society, and brought migrant workers into labor unions through aggressive organizing.[29] But doing so could have isolated migrants' economic function, as laborers, from their social quality. The migrant workers came to Korea primarily to work, but they also brought with them their social and cultural dimensions of their humanity. Labor organizers did not have the capacity to engage the public through citizen's education about difference, discrimination, and multiculturality; in short, the organizations like JCMK and other citizens groups laid the foundation for the kinds of labor organizing that was made possible later on. The Supreme Court decisions

---

[29]Lee, Yoon-Ju (2001), MWSH Executive Officer, takes this a step further by claiming that "the petit-bourgeois within the migrant labor movement arena seek to maintain dependent relationship between migrants and the organizations." She adds:

"since [advocacy organizations] want to see everything done within their control, they ultimately do not support migrant autonomy or unity even though they appear to endorse with a labor movement perspective."

regarding migrant worker rights partially reflect the societal trends; although it has taken some time to reach this decision, the Korean society is well prepared to embrace it without causing social division. It is worth noting again that no major decisions that extended benefits and rights to migrant populations invited hostility or opposition from prominent social or political groups in Korea.

Finally, Korea's trade unions have maintained resolute solidarity with migrant workers from the very beginning despite the overwhelming challenges of organizing across legal, cultural, and language barriers.[30] As unauthorized workers, they have had to contend with unpredictable crackdowns, illegal raids, and targeted arrests of their union leaders. In the end, they have managed to win some important victories, such as the industrial accident compensation, the abolition of the Industrial Trainee System, the three basic labor rights (collective bargaining, collective action, and labor union formation), and the rightful place in the hearts and minds of the progressive social movement and labor leaders. The support networks for migrant workers in Korea are wide and deep, and they can utilize the resources to expand upon their gains, so that they may secure greater freedoms pertaining to movement, residence, and employment. What has been less visible, but critical and invaluable, throughout the discussion about the role of labor unions, is international solidarity networks and the various international labor and human rights instruments. Korea's labor unions and CSOs frequently engage in international conferences about migrant labor issues and reference United Nation's and International Labour Organization's (ILO) instruments that serve as global standards for how host society ought to treat migrant workers and families. These resources provide the Korean practitioners and migrants alike with the language and conceptual framework to combat ethnocentrism and to achieve equality and basic human rights for all citizens.

[30]The article by Lim (2015) offers a good reflection of the meaning of the recent Supreme Court decision and the tasks ahead for maintaining solidarity between Korean and migrant workers.

Chapter 3

Sex Workers, Marriage Migrants, and Gender Formation in Migrant Advocacy

In a magazine article titled, "Liberal Feminism has a Sex Work Problem" (*New Republic*, October 2019) by Melissa Gira Grant, she opens with a rather jarring statement that the world's leading feminist organization, the National Organization for Women (NOW), opposes decriminalization of sex work. For many, such a political position seems out of step with its historical track record of fighting on behalf of women's rights that range from marriage and work-related legal rights to broad societal issues that structure inequality and violence toward women. The position, however, raises some unexamined questions and reveals intricate complexities regarding gender-based violence, agency, inequality, complicity, and responsibility. In South Korea, the influx of international women into its nightlife and sex industry similarly flares up dynamic discourses about the core issues pertaining to the preponderance of commodified sex, ways to reduce violence toward women engaged in sex work, and, more broadly, working toward achieving gender equality in all areas of public and private lives. Adding layers of complexity to these issues, the international marriage migrants who come from economically challenging countries to intermarry with rural Korean men draw out similar issues of vulnerability, structural violence, social inequality, and government complicity. In supporting international women, Korea's advocacy organizations have greatly expanded their outreach services with strong financial backing from the national government and have contributed meaningfully to public discourses about gender, and its intersection with ethnicity and nationalism. This chapter traces the gender formation[1] of migrant advocacy as it relates to international women in sex, entertainment, and marriage industries in South Korea.

---

[1]By gender formation, I refer to the process of social reproduction that transcends an individual identity, experience and perspective. Gender is intrinsically social and systemic in the way (1) both men and women acquire a roadmap for how to think and behave in particular social contexts; (2) the action contexts, though not completely predetermined, already embody socially ascribed meanings that inform the boundaries

Organized Labor and Civil Society for Multiculturalism:
A Solidarity Success Story from South Korea, 45–67

doi:10.1108/978-1-83982-388-620200003

Korea's Internationalization of Sex, Entertainment, and Marriage Industries: Gender Perspectives

The preponderance of international sex industry has generated a great deal of literature. From a structural perspective, the uneven development of countries provides the backdrop against which global sex trade unfolds. The fact that global inequalities disrupt established economic patterns, produce massive displacement of workers, and lead to migrations within and abroad has long been well documented (Portes, 1978; Sassen-Koob, 1981; Zolberg, 1979). Such structural conditions provide the push context for female-led migrations from rural areas to cities and eventually to foreign destinations. Complementing the structural analysis, other dimensions of international sex industry underscore the importance of networks, technology, and culture. These include the growth of international organizations for smuggling and trafficking women and children (Kangaspunta, 2003; McGill, 2003; Skrobanek, Boonpakdi & Janthakeero, 1997); the salience of crime groups, such as the snakeheads, the Russian mafias, and the *yakuza* (Matsui, 1999); the role of state and its systemic failure to monitor and break the chain of trafficking (Barry, 1995; Enloe, 1989; Jeffreys, 1999); the cultural complicity in tolerating forced or other forms of involuntary prostitution aided by rapid transportation and communication technologies (Campani, 1998; Cheng, 2000; O'Connell Davidson, 1998).

In examining the global significance of sex industry in South Korea, other studies have generally affirmed the conceptual frameworks of the existing literature on the topic. For instance, according to a study by International Organization for Migration (IOM, 2002), foreign women support the increasing demand in Korea's sex industry. The report shows that foreign women were recruited principally for the American military personnel due to a shortage of Korean women serving the military camp towns. The presence of foreign women in these areas symbolized the arrival of "a full-fledged international sex industry" (IOM, 2002, p. 25). But, this supply-and-demand argument is inadequate in explaining the speed with which the popularity of foreign women spread into non-military camp towns. The quick transition from primarily American to Korean clientele underlies the preexisting cultural and structural environment, which made the adaptation seamless and timely. In another study sponsored by the Ministry of Gender Equality (2003), Seol et al. showed four main causes of trafficking foreign women into sex and entertainment industry in South Korea.[2] First, the uneven development of countries within the world capitalist system and the commodification of sex set the context for funneling young women from less-developed countries

of acceptability; and (3) the agents reinforce the malleable structure of action through the routinized performatives.

[2]This study was based on interviews of 195 women, most of whom have come from the former Soviet Union countries (89) and the Philippines (106). Interviews and surveys were conducted for three months from August 25, 2003, to November 24, 2003. For additional information, see (Ministry of Gender Equality, 2004).

into South Korea. Second, the profit-seeking international manpower agencies and the clandestine organizations actively promote migration of women. Third, state policies and male-centered culture induce impoverished and unemployed women from overseas in search of better economic opportunities. Finally, the male-centered Korean society seeks to fulfill its need for women in the sex industry, and the government's tacit approval of such practice has contributed to the proliferation of international trafficking of women into South Korea.

While the structural and supply-and-demand explanations offer some valuable context for international women in the sex industry, the gender perspectives bring to the fore the salience of status and power that both reflect and configure an uneven process, policy, and interests. The gender perspectives, thus, approach international migration of women in the following ways: one, feminization of migration into service industries that provide care work reinforces uneven valuation of work based on gender (Chafetz, 1997; Hochschild, 2003), which suggests that the employment opportunity structure in both sending and receiving countries is gendered and stratified; two, "housewifization" fosters capital accumulation by rendering "women's work" "weak, dependent, and domesticated" (Mies, 1998, p. 40), which supports the idea that the public sphere is still predominantly the male domain where hetero-patriarchal power is reproduced; three, the preponderance of women in informal economies is both function and outcome of economic transformation that contributes toward gender segmentation and exploitation (Honig, 1998; Summerfield & Aslanbeigui, 1998); four, all migrations are inherently gendered as they reflect gender-segregated structures and mechanisms in both sending and host societies (De Los Reyes, 2001; Harzig, 2001); five, working class men derive advantages both within the household and in the labor force because women are overwhelmingly responsible for maintaining and reproducing unwaged labor force (Sacks, 1974; Shelton & Agger, 1993; Sokoloff, 1980); six, gender stratification systems accompany and simultaneously perform ideologies that naturalize difference and inequality (Blumberg, 1984); seven, migrant sending and receiving states respond to and support immigration frameworks that normalize violence on the basis of gender, class and ethnicity (Piper, 2003); eight, gender is an "emergent feature" of social situations, neither fixed in structure nor a set of individual traits (West & Fenstermaker, 1993, p. 151), thus subject to changes through performatives of individuals.

In view of the gender perspectives, the ensuing analysis focuses on the role of migrant women advocacy organizations in mediating the gender-based inequalities pertinent to international women in South Korea. The proliferation of organizations for international women also underlies the salience of race and ethnicity in framing public discourses, shaping social policies, and impacting working conditions in respective industries. It should be noted that women who work in the nightlife and entertainment industry cannot be compared to marriage migrants, *idem per idem*, since they encounter vastly different challenges, but the significant overlap in terms of the public discourses pertaining to the advocacy work of both groups of women supports the gender formation regarding immigrant women in Korea.

South Korea's Sex Industry

Prostitution, particularly the selling and buying of women's bodies for male pleasure, is an age-old social phenomenon across the globe. Korea is no exception in that the practice dates back hundreds of years (Soh, 2004), but the modern-day sex industry speaks to significant changes in social and economic structures that continue to support it. Since the Japanese colonization of Korea between 1910 and 1945, prostitution was "officially recognized, licensed, and even developed on a nationwide scale," and then the establishment of the US camptowns near the military bases drew significant demand immediately after the Korean War in 1953, despite some official efforts to abolish prostitution in the 1960s (IOM, 2002, p. 24). Many Korean women "served" to "comfort" these American GIs through the 1970s and 1980s, but the sex industry in Korea fundamentally changed beginning in the 1990s, corresponding with the burgeoning economic development, the rising wealth and standard of living, and the introduction of foreign labor and marriage migrants in Korean society. Several new developments accompanying these changes are worth highlighting: one, foreign women[3] started to replace Korean women who catered to American servicemen; two, the diversity of venues where sex is bought, sold, and trafficked simply exploded; and, three, the preponderance of sex industry in Korea underlies the evolving status of its supply and demand structure, where the advances in technology, particularly through the Internet and social media, aided in deepening and widening the market for sex. The rapid internationalization of Korea's sex industry not only reflects the diversification of the industry, but also premises the importance of ethnicity and race in marketing sex to Korean men.

In a comprehensive national study on the sex industry, the Ministry of Gender Equality and Family, in collaboration with the Korea Institute of Criminology (2002a), provided a shocking report that over 57,900 businesses were engaged in selling sex, employing some 330,000 women. Relative to the number of women working in traditional sex parlors and red-light districts, the number of women employed in businesses where sexual service is not their main function amounted to about 73% of the total (Table 3.1). These establishments varied greatly, including karaoke bars, massage parlors, room salons, public bath houses, barbershops, and hotels. Moreover, some have operated sex business by establishing fake companies, such as employment referral centers, marriage counseling offices, and special event planning offices. The rapid advances in technology and the Internet-based websites facilitated virtual encounters that became increasingly difficult to track the volume of the sex industry. Nonetheless, this report estimated that about US$24 billion worth of economic activities were generated from the sex industry, representing 4.1% of South Korea's gross domestic product (GDP). This figure surpassed the business activities of the nation's electricity, gas, and water (about 2.9% of GDP) and came close to the combined activities of agriculture, forestry,

---

[3]The foreign women come from diverse places, including Russia, the countries that once belonged to the former Soviet Union, the Philippines, China, and the Southeast Asian countries.

Table 3.1. Scope and Types of Sex Industry in Korea, 2002.

	Number of Workers	Number of Employers	Annual Business Activity (Thousand US$)
Traditional prostitution sites[a]	9,092	2,938	1,831,800
Prostitution as a side business[b]	241,114	57,938	16,496,600
Other methods[c]	79,012	19,224	5,787,900
Total	329,218	80,100	24,116,300

Source: Originally published in Kim and Fu (2008, p. 494).
Notes: [a]Traditional prostitution sites include the red-light districts and specific neighborhoods where prostitution is the main business. These are areas widely known by common people in Korea, which include Seoul Yongsan, Chungyangri 588, Youngdeungpo, Miari Texas, Pusan Wanwoldong, Incheon HakIkdong, etc.
[b]Prostitution as a side business denotes establishments that refer customers to sex workers if they specifically request such services, but their main businesses may be classified as serving foods and alcohol, public health, and hotel services (including saunas, public bathhouses, barbershops, massage parlors, and call massages on demand).
[c]Other methods range greatly, including fake businesses with physical buildings (such as employment referral services, marriage counseling offices, and special event planners) or direct contacts between sex workers and buyers (specifically catering to mountain climbers, drivers, elderly, American GIs, and Internet-based customers).

and fisheries, which generated about 4.4% of GDP (Kim & Fu, 2008, p. 494). On average, about 358,000 men participated in illicit sexual activities daily, and men aged between 20 and 64 years paid for sex about 4.5 times per month.[4] Five years later, in 2007, the follow-up study revealed that, while the total number of women sex workers and the traditional businesses have decreased, it was nearly impossible to assess the total volume of the industry since the business is constantly evolving and diversifying.[5] The Ministry of Gender and Family maintained its commitment to monitoring the sex industry and supported the issuance of comprehensive reports every three years, as stipulated in the revised law. Again, in 2016, the Ministry provided a comparative report, measuring the changes based on the 2010 and 2013 reports, and announced its tentative results, which invited criticism from some who argued that the traditional methods of marketing sex have waned but the new venues have been insufficiently addressed in the report.[6]

[4]"The economic activity of the sex industry at 24 trillion won annually." Retrieved from http://www.donga.com/news/article/all/20030205/7909586/1.
[5]Retrieved from https://news.naver.com/main/read.nhn?mode=LSD&mid=sec&sid1=102&oid=001&aid=0002274066. Accessed on February 15, 2020.
[6]See, for instance, the article in *Donga Ilbo* where the reporter charged that the Ministry failed to account for the many ways in which the sex industry has evolved since

In its periodic report on the United Nations Convention on the Elimination of All Forms of Discrimination against Women (CEDAW, 2011, p. 115), the Korean Women's Association United,[7] comprising of some 33 regional centers and organizations, identified Korea's E-6-2 visa system as the principal gateway through which foreign women were trafficked into Korea's sex industry and urged the government to "strictly administer and manage the Korean agencies for foreign entertainers and the entertainment establishments hiring foreign women." Indeed, one of the first overseas entertainers to work in Korea occurred in the early 1990s. Following the collapse of Communism in Eastern Europe, experienced ballerinas, gymnasts, and acrobats from Russia, Ukraine, Moldova, and other countries began performing in Korea's amusement parks. More importantly, the Korean government's liberalization of the E-6 visa category in 1998 allowed the Korean Media Rating Board to oversee performer contracts of thousands of entertainers. In response, the number of performance planning agencies increased from only 14 in 1998 to 157 by 2002, and concomitantly the number of E-6 visa holders skyrocketed from 595 in 1995 to over 8,500 in 2001 (Kim & Fu, 2008). The sudden increase in the number of such agencies underscores the popularity of international women in entertainment businesses, which expanded beyond daytime performances in amusement parks into nightlife industries. The great majority of the women entered Korea voluntarily in order to perform as singers and dancers, but their circumstances changed once they were introduced

---

the amended law was passed in 2004. In particular, the reporter argued that the sex business is indeed quite vibrant with the development of new modes of soliciting prostitution, including private officetels (small studio rooms), kiss rooms, lip cafés, ear cleaning rooms, call girls, and Internet chat rooms. These venues have literally exploded, while the government report lagged behind in tracking the new methods and trends. http://www.donga.com/news/article/all/20170502/84167233/1. Accessed February 15, 2020.

[7]The member organizations include: Kyunggi Women's Association United, Kyungnam Women's Association United, Gwanggju Jonnam Women's Association United, Daegu Kyungbuk's Women's Association United, Busan Women's Association United, Jonbuk Women's Association United, Kyungnam Women's Association, Korean Association of Christian Women for Women Minjung, Daegu Women's Association, Daejun Women's Association, Busan Counseling Center Against Sexual Violence, Busan Women Education Center, Korean Catholic Women's Community for a New World, Seumter, National Solidarity for the Solution for Sexual Trafficking, Suwon Women's Association, Korea Women's Center for Social Research, Ulsan Women's Association, Jeju Women's Association, Jeju Association for Women's Rights, National Association of Parent's for Charm/Education, Chungbuk Women's Association, Pohang Women's Association, Women Making Peace, Korea Sexual Violence Relief Center, Korea Women Workers Association, Korean Womenlink, Korea Women's Studies Institute, Korea Women's Hot Line, Korea Differently Abled Women United, Korean Association of Women Theologians, Korea Women Migrants' Human Rights Center, House Wives Meeting Together.

to bars, dance halls, and other venues where they were constantly pressured to sell their bodies for sex. Between 2000 and 2005, the top three countries with the highest number of E-6 and C-4 visas were issued to the Russia Federation (15,658), the Philippines (8,950), and Uzbekistan (1,948).[8] Initially, the Filipinas were recruited to work in the bars and dance halls in the American military camptowns, presumably because of their English proficiency and the declining number of Korean women working in these areas. Between 2006 and 2017, some 22,878 Filipinas entered Korea through the E-6 visa, followed by 2,780 women from China, 1,411 from Ukraine, and 1,068 from the Russia Federation (Table 3.2).

The Korean Institute of Criminology (KIC, 2011) also reported that, in addition to the E-6 visas, they identified two other methods by which foreign women may have been cornered into the sex industry. The first group of women entered Korea through temporary work visas, but, for a variety of reasons including the workplace abuse by their employers and Korean co-workers, they decided to leave factories and other places of employment in violation of the immigration laws. Their unauthorized visa status, combined with their financial exigencies, prompted many to turn to the entertainment and sex industry. The second group of women represented a portion of the "marriage migrants" whose real purpose was to work and make money in Korea. The marriage broker agencies may bring women in through fake marriages where women may have been completely fooled into paper marriages, but, in many cases, women have full knowledge of the situation and pay appropriate fees to brokers and fake husbands in order to enter Korea. Among some marriage migrants, Korean men took trips to the source countries and handpicked their wives from a line-up. The KIC report (2011) commented that such a practice is qualitatively very similar to the "mail-order brides" phenomenon where men from primarily advanced economies ordered brides from less-developed countries through catalogs. The number of marriage migrants exploded in the past decade, with an attendant increase in diversification of countries. China, Vietnam, and the Philippines showed the highest number of married women migrants between 2011 and 2017, but Table 3.3 also shows significant increases among other countries. In particular, the number of marriages with women from Uzbekistan consistently maintained about 1,100 cases per year from 2012 to 2017. For the same period, the annual average figures for women from Mongolia (1,314), Cambodia (2,842), and Thailand (2,237) showed measurable increases (Table 3.4). When many of the fake and semi-forced marriages break down, the women experience legal and financial vulnerabilities in a country where opportunities for gainful employment, other than sex work, may be very limited.

---

[8]The C-4 visas are for temporary employment of less than 90 days in entertainment, sports, modeling, fashion, lecture, research, and technical instruction; whereas the E-6 category is for similar areas that require more than 90 days of work.

Table 3.2. E-6 Entertainment Visas by Select Countries and Sex, 2006–2017.

		2006	2007	2008	2009	2010	2011	2012	2013	2014	2015	2016	2017	Total	% Female
Philippines	M	410	344	331	251	240	244	239	168	296	253	256	177	3209	
	F	1,499	1,567	2,001	2,254	1,762	1,075	1,496	1,441	2,935	2,743	2,270	1,835	22,878	87.7
Russia Fed	M	74	54	79	84	72	92	49	38	23	23	28	24	640	
	F	192	126	122	132	79	80	90	56	41	54	53	43	1,068	62.5
Ukraine	M	125	78	101	49	87	83	55	98	43	73	73	68	933	
	F	168	132	197	94	108	101	20	150	74	140	125	102	1,411	60.2
Bulgaria	M	48	32	29	15	8	3	1	5	1	2	2	1	147	
	F	54	26	28	12	11	7	6	7	5	4	3	0	163	52.6
Belarus	M	31	14	13	11	4	0	26	6	3	5	7	11	131	
	F	26	25	15	12	7	0	9	13	5	14	13	26	165	55.7
Kyrgyzstan	M	7	0	1	0	3	1	1	5	8	7	6	9	48	
	F	22	0	1	0	0	4	2	43	57	54	54	23	260	84.4
Uzbekistan	M	14	4	8	11	12	41	20	81	11	11	7	10	230	
	F	52	20	11	13	5	13	17	17	20	34	26	13	241	51.2
China	M	229	121	227	270	274	361	335	453	189	187	144	142	2,932	
	F	295	181	361	259	273	291	251	313	185	138	119	114	2,780	48.7
Indonesia	M	0	2	0	0	0	0	125	1	1	1	2	3	135	
	F	11	2	0	0	9	23	70	32	58	57	53	43	358	72.6
Thailand	M	3	10	9	10	15	6	5	48	26	16	6	8	162	
	F	0	4	2	1	3	15	9	23	13	15	12	11	108	40.0

Source: Ministry of Justice. Bureau of Immigration, Korea. Annual Statistical Report, Foreigner Policy, various years.

Table 3.3. F6 Marriage Migrants Visas by Select Countries and Sex, 2011–2017.

		2011	2012	2013	2014	2015	2016	2017	Total	% Female
China	M	289	2,754	7,641	3,873	3,830	8,565	9,543	36,495	
	F	1,595	18,097	36,589	22,606	21,151	38,202	39,045	177,285	82.9
Korean–Chinese	M	2	5,896	279	6,509	6,201	379	582	19,848	
	F	12	13,788	456	13,859	12,470	754	1,234	42,573	68.2
Taiwan	M	14	34	288	55	52	269	300	1,012	
	F	31	246	959	494	567	1,709	2,112	6,118	85.8
Thailand	M	2	35	60	66	70	75	100	408	
	F	38	1,202	1,563	1,944	2,083	2,799	3,829	13,458	97.1
Philippines	M	5	181	187	283	281	269	350	1,556	
	F	196	5,788	5,105	9,920	9,833	6,788	7,464	45,094	96.7
Vietnam	M	3	212	270	584	844	1,245	1,637	4,795	
	F	862	23,484	19,797	35,615	36,317	25,831	29,317	171,223	97.3
Indonesia	M	2	31	29	64	65	79	89	359	
	F	11	228	236	418	446	377	448	2,164	85.8
Mongolia	M	2	53	65	76	99	101	111	507	
	F	37	1,101	1,213	1,693	1,589	1,091	1,197	7,921	94.0
Uzbekistan	M	3	41	57	64	64	67	61	357	
	F	20	1,054	993	1,565	1,424	901	913	6,870	95.1
Cambodia	M	0	5	10	17	44	46	87	209	
	F	94	2,661	1,955	4,198	4,101	2,085	2,053	17,147	98.8
Nepal	M	5	90	68	127	118	63	79	550	
	F	18	545	304	854	779	186	223	2,909	84.1
Bangladesh	M	13	197	147	251	245	163	196	1,212	
	F	1	31	11	45	50	37	33	208	14.6
Pakistan	M	22	504	508	679	654	584	602	3,553	
	F	1	42	48	88	102	46	54	381	9.7

Source: Ministry of Justice. Bureau of Immigration, Korea. Annual Statistical Report, Foreigner Policy, various years.

Notes: The visa category F-6 was created in 2011 in order to facilitate their adaptation into Korean society through support and management.

Table 3.4. Interethnic Marriages from Select Countries, 2000–2018.

	2000–2002	2003–2005	2006–2008	2009–2011	2012–2014	2015–2017	2018	Total
Total interethnic marriages	41,330	101,772	112,523	97,297	77,604	62,700	22,698	515,924
Foreign Brides	27,327	74,575	86,408	73,681	55,096	44,368	16,608	378,063
Chinese	17,566	52,418	42,253	28,536	18,579	12,623	3,671	175,646
Vietnamese	685	9,685	25,020	24,508	17,099	15,392	6,338	98,727
Filipinas	2,514	2,855	4,471	5,621	5,038	2,712	852	24,063
Japanese	2,210	2,536	3,413	3,457	3,872	2,711	987	19,186
Cambodians	5	248	2,857	3,017	1,824	1,470	455	9,876
Thai	749	935	1,428	1,288	1,053	2,280	1,560	9,293
USA	760	948	1,051	1,351	1,799	1,688	567	8,164
Other	2,462	3,565	4,055	4,925	5,349	5,492	2,178	28,026
Foreign Husbands	14,003	27,197	26,115	23,616	22,508	18,332	6,090	137,861
Japanese	7,326	8,791	9,504	6,221	4,124	1,500	313	37,779
China	695	9,845	7,176	6,779	5,303	4,420	1,489	35,707
USA	3,401	3,946	4,124	4,460	5,096	4,381	1,439	26,847
Canadians	486	729	1,052	1,183	1,461	1,299	402	6,612
Australians	246	342	459	569	777	654	189	3,236
Other	1,148	2,495	2,655	3,174	4,834	6,078	2,258	22,642

Source: Statistics Korea, "Annual Population Statistics," 2000–2018.

Marriage Migration to Korea

The influx of international women into the nightlife industry in the mid-1990s coincided with a steady increase in the number of international marriages. The popularity of interethnic marriages was very surprising since Korea had promoted itself as a homogeneous society and frowned on such ethnic unions largely due to the prevalence of Korean women marrying American GIs.[9] Several factors intersecting in the post-1990s, however, contributed to not only wide acceptance of such unions, but also an active promotion by both the government and private sectors. Some of these influences include the shortage of marriageable women in rural communities, the influx of international women into Korean society and the subsequent expansion of advocacy and religious organizations in support of such women, the government support for interethnic marriages and the private sector seeking to profit from such ventures, and the overall internationalization of the Korean population due to the frequency of international travel, the various media coverage of interethnic couples, and the promotion of multicultural policies and programs at all levels.

As the Korean society experienced a rapidly aging population, it also accompanied the low fertility and marriage rates especially in rural communities. Various governments at the regional and city levels began to promote international marriages by offering financial and non-pecuniary incentives.[10] In the Mu Joo County in the North Chonla Province, for instance, the Provincial Government had announced its plan to set aside 50 million won (US$50,000) in order to help defray the cost associated with international marriages by paying for the airfare and other expenses for ten eligible rural men. A few months later, its neighboring County of Im Sil submitted a plan to support rural men in their communities by earmarking 40 million won (US$40,000) for the effort, recognizing that each international marriage requires about US$7,000 to US$15,000. The Budget Officer of the County added that the single males growing older in rural communities presented a major social problem and vowed to deal with such a challenge by working together with the City Board, the City Finance Office, and the social service organizations.[11] In 2000, the total number of interethnic marriages

---

[9]See the article by Moon (2007) regarding the perception of Korean women serving American GIs in the military camptowns throughout the military regime period from the 1960s to the 1990s.

[10]The national campaign to support marriages of rural men started in the late-1980s. Representative Ki-gap Kang, a Democratic Labor Party member of Korea's National Assembly, had begun an effort to marry rural men by taking them up into the cities where the eligible women had moved *en masse*. The idea of intermarrying Korean men with international women still lay dormant but the influx of foreign women through various channels fundamentally changed how aging men solicited women beyond the ethnic and national borders. See the article, https://news.sbs.co.kr/news/endPage.do?news_id=N1000412047&plink=OLDURL.

[11]See the following articles: https://news.naver.com/main/read.nhn?mode=LSD&mid=sec&sid1=102&oid=003&aid=0000171797; https://news.naver.com/main/read.nhn?mode=LSD&mid=sec&sid1=102&oid=021&aid=0000175471.

amounted to 11,605 (or 3.49 %) of 332,090 total marriages. The interethnic marriages peaked at 42,356 cases (or 13.48%) in 2005 and then tapered off at about 30,000 (or 10.5%) in 2011 and about 22,700 (or 8.8%) in 2018 (Table 3.5).

Based on the Annual Population Data regarding interethnic marriages, several important patterns emerged: one, the interethnic marriages contributed to the internationalization of rural communities, which contrasts against the international women in entertainment industries where they are likely to be located in metropolitan areas; two, over time the countries represented by the marriage women migrants diversified; three, Korean women marrying foreign men from Islamic countries, such as Pakistan and Bangladesh, showed a steady increase; finally, the overall level of interethnic marriages currently constitute a significant portion all marriages, especially in light of the overall decline in the number of total marriages reflecting in part the low fertility rate and the increasingly aging Korean society. The role of immigrant women appears imminent and critical in the next few decades.

Government Policies Toward Marriage Migrants and International Sex Workers

Recognizing the increasing importance of interethnic marriages, the central government of Korea began working on developing institutional and legal frameworks to support, protect, and assimilate international women into Korean society. Incidentally, during the same period, the government sought to protect the victims of prostitution by passing a few critical laws aimed at criminalizing the traffickers and facilitators of sex work while decriminalizing the women who may have been coerced into prostitution. The lawmakers were careful to point out the layers of vulnerabilities of international women who experience difficulties not only because of their gender, but also because of their legal status, national origin, language barriers, and cultural challenges.

In the summer of 2004, the process for supporting the marriage migrants began with the financial contribution from Korea's largest makeup company, Taepyungyang Hwahak (Pacific Chemical).[12] The Ministry of Gender Equality, which was formed just three years prior under the progressive Kim Dae-Jung presidency, worked in concert with the Office for Government Policy Coordination under the direction of the Prime Minister. As its first project, the Ministry of Gender Equality[13] entrusted the Women Migrants' Human Rights Center of Korea with the responsibility of administering Korean language and marriage migrant support programs. The organization began modestly with only five support centers nationally, but, in the following months, various government ministries under

[12]The name of the company changed to Amore Pacific Corporation in June 2006. The amount of support was reportedly US$1 million, divided into five installments of US$200,000 for the next five years.

[13]The reconstitution of the ministries occurred in 2010; the Ministry of Gender Equality changed to the Ministry of Gender Equality and Family.

Table 3.5. Marriages and Interethnic Marriages in Korea, 2008–2018.

	2008	**2009**	**2010**	**2011**	**2012**	**2013**	**2014**	**2015**	**2016**	**2017**	**2018**	%
Total marriages	327.7	309.8	326.1	329.1	327.1	322.8	305.5	302.8	281.6	264.5	257.6	100
Total interethnic marriages	36.2	33.3	34.2	29.8	28.3	26	23.3	21.3	20.6	20.8	22.7	8.8
	11.0%	10.7%	10.5%	9.1%	8.7%	8.1%	7.6%	7.0%	7.3%	7.9%	8.8%	
Marriages with non-Korean women	28.2	25.1	26.3	22.3	20.6	18.3	16.2	14.7	14.8	14.9	16.6	6.4
	77.9%	75.4%	76.9%	74.8%	72.8%	70.4%	69.5%	69.0%	71.8%	71.6%	73.1%	
Marriages with non-Korean men	8	8.2	8	7.5	7.7	7.7	7.2	6.6	5.8	6	6.1	2.4
	22.1%	24.6%	23.4%	25.2%	27.2%	29.6%	30.9%	31.0%	28.2%	28.8%	26.9%	

Source: Statistics Korea, "Marriage and Divorce Statistics," 2019.

President Roh Moo-hyun established the Discrimination Remedy Committee and began to address the common concerns impacting marriage migrants in a much more systematic way. In the following two years, the National Assembly first amended the Basic Social Security Law in order to support the multicultural families, established shelters exclusively for marriage migrants who fell victim to domestic abuse and conducted a study in the source countries where women are selected for marriages. More importantly, the expansion of government involvement in marriage migrants culminated in the passage of the Multicultural Family Support Law in 2007 (Han, 2010).

The basic motivation of the Multicultural Family Support Law was to promote stable family life and to encourage social integration of marriage migrants. Toward this end, the provisions of the Law specified the following: to provide basic informational and educational materials about life in Korea (Article 6), to make available family counseling and parenthood educational programs (Article 7), to offer pre- and postnatal care by referring them to specialists (Article 9), and to provide easy access to local organizations where translation and interpretation services may be rendered (Article 11). In fulfilling these mandates, the Ministry of Health, Welfare and Family Affairs was charged with creating the "Multicultural Family Support Centers" throughout Korea. Currently, there are 218 centers in all of the major cities and townships, offering a variety of educational, medical, counseling, and parental services in 13 different languages.[14] The expansive scope of government-run Multicultural Family Support Centers is impressive, but it presents significant challenges to non-government organizations (NGO) in maintaining autonomy, financially and ideologically, and sustaining critical perspectives concerning the government's tendencies to control, manage, and discipline the public (Cha, 2010).

Spearheading the government's effort to socially integrate marriage migrants, the Ministry of Gender Equality simultaneously, in the same year, sought to transform the nation's sex industry. In 2004, the National Assembly passed two laws aimed at curbing demand for prostitution by targeting punishment toward brokers and employers, while protecting the victims of forced prostitution.[15] This was a significant departure from the previous law, which categorized all sex work as an "immoral act," subjecting women to punishment and social stigmatization.[16] While the new law did not decriminalize sex work, it redefined the women who may have been coerced into sex work as "victims" who require state protection and support. Toward this end, the law facilitated the women to break the chain of indentured servitude by nullifying any contract or debenture between employers and sex workers. The impetus for the new laws started two years prior,

[14]The languages include Korean, English, Chinese, Vietnamese, Japanese, Tagalog, Khmer, Uzbek, Laos, Russian, Thai, Mongolian, and Nepalese. As of March 2010, the Ministry of Gender Equality and Family has been overseeing policies pertaining to family issues, including the operation of the Multicultural Family Support Centers.

[15]Retrieved from http://www.law.go.kr/법령/성매매알선등행위의처벌에관한법률/(07196,20040322).

[16]Retrieved from https://terms.naver.com/entry.nhn?docId=1133206&cid=40942&categoryId=31708.

in January 2002, when 14 women died from a fire in their place of work where they were forcibly quartered in squalid, padlocked rooms. Although the fire was put out in 24 minutes, the women inside the locked rooms had no way of escaping. Some of the women kept diaries where they had lamented over mundane things that they were prohibited from doing, such as being able to freely go to a supermarket or a public bathhouse or coffee shops. It was also revealed that the owner of the establishment had regularly paid bribes to local police officers. This establishment was located about 100 m from the police station.[17]

Shortly thereafter, the Korean National Council of Women, the largest women's organization in Korea, established a Special Committee for Amending the Anti-Prostitution Law. Their work culminated in not only the passage of the relevant laws, but also an important court decision.[18] As stated in its syllabus, the primary objective of the new law was to protect women, to decrease their participation in sex work, and to punish the brokers and employers of sex work. In fulfilling its stated purpose, the new law compelled the government to take a much more proactive role in preventing prostitution, protecting the victims, supporting their recovery and eventual independence, and establishing necessary legal and institutional mechanisms in support of these activities. Specifically, the law stipulated that the government shall establish a system of reporting prostitution and its related activities, conduct research and provide public education, establish and operate facilities in support of protecting victims and their self-reliance, provide shelters and employment training, establish a system of collaboration across allied government agencies, monitor areas and environments contributing to prostitution, and, finally, the government shall strive to improve international cooperation in order to prevent human trafficking for prostitution.[19]

Consolidation and Gender Formation of Advocacy Organizations

The progressive movements within the ranks of civil society organizations reflect a complex web of history that extends beyond the advocacy work regarding migrant women and sex workers. Tracing these intersecting currents requires an analysis of Korea's modern-day women's movement history, which has been significantly shaped by the evolving political landscape since the post-Korean-War-period

[17]Retrieved from http://www.womennews.co.kr/news/articleView.html?idxno=195894.

[18]In July 2002, the Seoul Central District Court ruled that the employers were responsible for the death of sex workers who died in another fire in Kunsan Daemyungdong two years earlier. They were ordered to pay 5.9 billion Korean won (about US$590,000), and the Court also pointed out that the government was also responsible for not acting properly in a timely manner to intervene on behalf of the women who were locked in their rooms. The government was ordered to compensate 67 million won (US$67,000) to the plaintiffs. See the article, https://news.naver.com/main/read.nhn?mode=LSD&mid=sec&sid1=102&oid=047&aid=0000007629. Accessed on February 16, 2020.

[19]Retrieved from http://www.law.go.kr/법령/성매매방지및피해자보호등에관한법률/(07212,20040322).

and, more significantly, by the internationalization of basic and human rights standards. These influences dynamically filter through various government, quasi-government, and non-government entities. The public discourses, too, follow closely these patterns of internationalization, and the advocacy work for (or with), including the politically preferred language, migrant women and international sex workers simultaneously reflect and reinforce such standards of engagement. Even though Korea's social movement is characterized by dynamism and its unique historiography, the ideological continuity across diverse segments of the Korean society demonstrates an articulation of global standards for women's rights and issues, including migrant women as wives and sex workers. The consolidation of advocacy work is, thus, structured through the pre-existing structures of institutions at the local, regional, national, and international levels. This is particularly true among the liberal democracies that share a common set of beliefs about basic human rights, particularly those groups that have been identified as society's vulnerable populations, including the diversity of minorities and women. Thus, the reproduction of global standards at the local level, facilitated by legal mandates and multilevel organizational structures, mutually contribute toward the globally resonant gender formation of advocacy organizations.

While there are numerous organizations working on issues pertaining to marriage migrants, and international sex workers in Korea, the advocacy discourse gets shaped through several key stakeholders that generate standards and frameworks, share knowledge through various venues, and disseminate information to the general public via national laws, educational programs, and theme-specific campaigns. At the core of such mechanisms lies the United Nations Human Rights instruments to which the Republic of Korea is a signatory to some foundational conventions, including the International Covenant on Civil and Political Rights (CCPR), Convention on the Elimination of All Forms of Discrimination against Women (CEDAW), International Convention on the Elimination of All Forms of Racial Discrimination (CERD), and International Covenant on Economic, Social and Cultural Rights (CESCR). At the national level, the National Human Rights Commission of Korea serves as the main vehicle through which it educates, monitors, and analyzes the level of observance of the various international instruments.[20] Established in 2001, the Commission was created through the National Human Rights Commission Act, which defines as its mission,

> to contribute to the embodiment of human dignity and worth as well as to the safeguard of the basic order of democracy ... and to ensure that inviolable, fundamental human right of all individuals are protected and the standards of human rights are improved.[21]

---

[20]International Organization for Migration (IOM) has a national office in Korea, which systematically collects and reports on the development of policies and treatment regarding international migrant and minority populations.

[21]Retrieved from https://www.humanrights.go.kr/site/homepage/menu/viewMenu?menuid=002001001001. Accessed on March 2, 2020.

Toward this end, the Commission's mandate establishes the global–local connection by developing human rights policies, investigating discrimination and human rights violations, monitoring national implementation of international human rights treaties, and collaborating with government, civil society, and UN bodies in an effort to protect and promote human rights.

Civil society organizations (CSOs) play a pivotal role as an intermediary between the international bodies and local communities, thereby providing both top–down and ground–up information to respective constituents (Fig. 3.1). Some of these organizations have secured the General or Special Consultative Status with the United Nations Human Rights Commission. This allows such organizations to provide critical feedback in the form of raising a list of issues for the government through formal communication with the relevant Commissions, assessing the progress by monitoring policy changes in accordance with the country reports, and

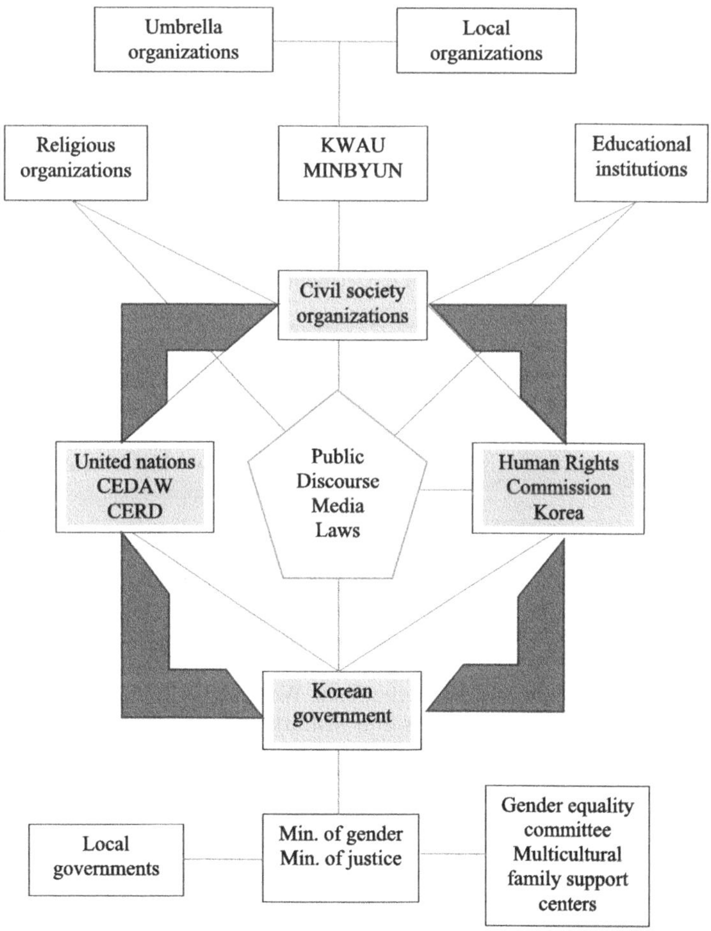

Fig. 3.1. Key Stakeholders of Marriage Migrants and International Sex Workers.

networking with local, regional, and national organizations that administer services to affected populations. The Korea Women's Associations United (KWAU) represents one such organization that serves as an interlocutor for numerous NGOs at CEDAW, with the goal of advancing the status of women and dismantling the age-old patriarchal laws and traditions.[22] In 1997, the organization helped to successfully amend the Nationality Law, which granted the right of women to pass on maternal lineage to their children. For the first time in Korea's history, a child born between a non-Korean father and a Korean mother was permitted to retain the Korean citizenship.[23] Utilizing international conventions to put pressure on the government did not occur easily or automatically. Speaking on the "First CEDAW Impact Study," Youngsook Cho, the KWAU Director, confided that even in the late-1990s women activists in Korea had little knowledge about CEDAW until two activists from the organization fortuitously attended a "monitor training program co-hosted by UNIFEM and IWRAW" (Y. Cho, 2010).[24] Upon their return to Korea, the two activists immediately organized a training session to its 28 member organizations and, in 1998, KWAU submitted its first Civil Society Organization Shadow Report at the 19th session of the CEDAW (Y. Cho, 2010, p. 190). Accompanying Y. Cho, Dr. Hoo-jung Yoon, the newly appointed Chairperson of the Presidential Commission on Women's Affairs, which was a precursor to the Ministry of Gender Equality, and Ms. Heisoo Shin, the President of Women's Hot Line, helped to organize women's groups in order to "secure the implementation of the CEDAW in Korea" (Y. Cho, 2010, p. 191).

In collaboration with KWAU, another organization with Special Consultative Status at the United Nations Department of Economic and Social Affairs is MINBYUN, the Lawyers for a Democratic Society. In its latest Alternative Report to the UN Committee on the Elimination of Racial Discrimination (CERD), the organization collaborated with GongGam, the Human Rights Law Foundation, and GAMDONG, the Immigrants Advocacy Center, and with over 100 CSOs in putting together the report at its 97th session. Some of these organizations are very well-established umbrella groups that work in concert with local

[22]Korea's Family Law is a prime example of the patriarchal tradition in that women are compelled by law to move her family register to her husband's upon marriage. This law was amended in 1991seven years after the ratification of CEDAW.

[23]See J. Kim (2005, pp. 390–396) for a discussion on the role of women's organizations and the evolution of Korea's Nationality Act.

[24]IWRAW-Asia Pacific signifies International Women's Rights Action Watch that seeks to "disrupt structures, systems and institutions that violate women's human rights … and engage in movement building that amplifies women's voices and activism to create alternative political narratives and spaces." UNIFEM, now UN Women, is an acronym for (in French) United Nations Development Fund for Women, which was created to"support countries that have limited resources for carrying out their national plans and programs for the advancement of women and for the implementation of the Objectives of the International Women's Year adopted by the World Conference of the International Women's Year, held at Mexico City in 1975" (UN General Assembly, 1976).

and regional centers who work directly with various migrant populations and their families.[25] These organizations, among many, include Joint Committee with Migrants in Korea, Women Migrants Human Rights Center, and the National Solidarity against Sexual Exploitation of Women. Because of their strong local-to-global networks, many of the practitioners who may not have had an opportunity to attend any of the UN sessions are familiar with the various UN protocols through trainings, forums, and praxis. Supporting the efforts of CSOs, numerous independent researchers and academics from major universities throughout Korea engage in broad discourses about human rights as framed through the UN Conventions and specific issues pertaining to feminism, migration, and human trafficking. The collaborative structure of these organizations contributes toward streamlining perspectives and messages regarding key issues, including marriage migrants, and international sex workers.

Gendered Discourse Regarding Marriage Migrants and International Sex Workers

Various advocates of marriage migrants and sex workers articulate a consistent message where women have been uniformly described as victims of patriarchy, as manifested in laws, cultures, and mores that reflect sexist, misogynistic, and culturally-racist views, attitudes, and practices. Clearly, many women have been victimized by unscrupulous brokers, opportunistic business operators, and national laws that fail to close the loopholes and protect vulnerable women. Such systemic issues are complex and difficult to disentangle, but, even more so if the women do not consider themselves as victims or fail to see any viable alternatives. The tension between the established advocacy discourse and the realities of women in presumably vulnerable positions raises a thorny dilemma that challenges taken-for-granted assumptions.

Speaking at a symposium, the Director of Seoul Migrant Women Counseling Center lamented that the divorce rate among marriage migrants is relatively higher than the national average, and it can be attributed to the instability of multicultural families and the lack of the Korean society's receptivity toward multiculturalism. "Despite the amount of attention and support for the multicultural families in the past ten years," she noted, "the difficulties they encounter due to their foreigner status is unimaginable" (Kang, 2015, p. 22). Representing GongGam, a public-interest law firm that collaborated with KWAU in preparing reports to CEDAW, Esquire Ra-mi So echoed this view and added the following fundamental problems with international marriages. To begin, the Korean society is not yet structurally prepared to receive international marriage migrants, given the inadequacies of legal frameworks in addressing the preponderance of domestic

[25]Other key organizations include the Korea Center for United Nations Human Rights Policy, Migrant Health Association in Korea, Korean Confederation of Trade Unions, Solidarity for Asian Human Rights and Culture, and Advocates for Public Interest Law.

violence and other forms of human rights violations. Second, the brokers exploit international women's vulnerabilities and unabashedly advertise women as commodities to be purchased at the pleasure of Korean men. Utilizing explicitly sexist and culturally-racist language, the brokers engage in unethical practices in order to generate demand among a diverse group of men who buy into commodified womanhood. Third, referring to banners that advertise international marriages, the esquire stated the central issues in the following way:

> The manner in which the brokers were able to capitalize on variously marginalized populations, including people with physical disabilities and older men, relies on the structural marginality of Vietnam within the global system, the bartering of commodified women's bodies in the global marketplace for marriages, the deeply embedded Korean patriarchal ideology about the purity and sanctity of women's sexuality, and the permissibility of commodified sexual encounters in the context of the marriage institution.

Such structures foster the idea that men in Korea can purchase women on demand, and, more importantly, the government is overtly supporting the commodification of international women and cornering the Korean men into the international marriage market that mirrors trafficking of society's vulnerable populations. In short, the international marriage migrants represent Korea's "human rights standard" because of their triple marginality as poor, women migrants (So, 2007).

In its oral statement to CEDAW, Ms. Cho, the director of KWAU, stated a view that is commonly shared across many of the organizations that currently advocate for marriage migrants and international sex workers. She articulated: "Gender social norms in the Korean society have been sturdily built up based on the deeply embedded culture of patriarchy and militarism" (CEDAW, 2017). She further stipulated that

> the mandatory trainings on the prevention of violence against women ... should cover a broader scope of manifestations... and their structural root causes ... in line with universal human rights standards and gender-related principles (CEDAW, 2017).

At a conference commemorating the tenth anniversary of the 2004 Revised Statute on prostitution, Hee-jung Kim, the Minister of Gender Equality and Family, stated unequivocally that "prostitution must be eliminated because it is an act that fundamentally violates one's human dignity." "Human beings," she added, "under no circumstance should ever be subjected to buying and selling of their bodies for money." In alignment with the Minister's perspective, the focus of the conference came together under the three themes: prevention, protection, and prosecution. The 2004 Revised Statute came about in response to the public outcry after the fire that killed 14 women trapped in their quarter. Feminist organizations, progressive churches, and civil society organizations successfully came together and pressured the government to revise the Anti-Prostitution law, with a focus on punishing the procurers, employers, and facilitators.[26] The Revised Statute would spare women who have been forced into prostitution; however, it still left intact the provision that criminalized prostitution. This is precisely because "prostitution is defined as a gendered violence and sexual exploitation against women," (CEDAW, 2018, p. 16) regardless of women's consent. The group called Migrant-Women-Human-Rights Solidarity affirmed this view and defined the migrant women in entertainment services as people who occupy the outermost ring of human rights violations. "As a first step," K. Lee (2001, p. 5) proclaimed, "women should approach the issues from a gendered perspective." This standpoint allows one to see the impact of military culture and male-centered patriarchal Korean society from a fresh lens and, from thence, a new movement's direction must be established. Furthermore, she advocates for the establishment of various feminist organizations working together in order to monitor and prevent transnational capital from inflicting violence against women. Finally, it is critical that

> we raise women's consciousness in order to instill in them the basic importance of human dignity ... and to continue the effort in empowering the most marginalized migrant women, so that they would be able to assert their rights on their own (K. Lee, 2001, p. 6).

Prostitution as inherently exploitive of women's sexuality is not new.[27] When women are structurally coerced into making decisions to sell their bodies for male pleasure, the act cannot be perceived as a demonstration of free will. Such a

---

[26]The National Solidarity for Resolving the Prostitution Problem (*sungmaemae munjae haegyuleul uihan jeonguk yeondae*) was created in response to two Kunsan fires in 2000 and 2002. It is the largest anti-prostitution consortium in Korea and its mission parallels that of the Ministry of Gender Equality and Family. This organization works in concert with KWAU for preparing its UN CEDAW reports. It is important to note also, in July 2001, the United States Department of State's human trafficking report on Korea embarrassed the nation as it received the lowest third tier rating among the 82 nations. It signaled Korea as both the source and transit country of human trafficking for the purpose of prostitution (KIC, 2002b).

[27]Among many, Kathleen Barry's work (1995) delineates a feminist perspective that establishes links across structural, global systems theory with patriarchy. The argument is somewhat linear and flattens complex issues into a simplified process: the development of industries fundamentally alters the family structures and fosters rural-to-urban migrations; women's marginal position in society renders their work less valuable and creates an economic structure that compels them to migrate from rural to urban centers and eventually overseas; the exacerbation of economic opportunities in cities siphons women into prostitution both domestically and internationally. This condition is fundamentally structural and, thus, the development of sex industry is a manifestation of a global capitalist system, rooted in economic, racial, and gendered exploitation.

perspective is widely shared among feminists and civil society advocates for international women in Korean society. At the "Sex Equality Forum" sponsored by KWAU, a representative from MINBYUN discussed a recent case involving a prostituted woman who filed a suit in the Constitutional Court in an effort to repeal the 2004 Revised Statute on prostitution, which still criminalized sex workers.[28] In response to a claim that voluntary prostitution is a "victimless crime," she argued that there are victims because "it is entirely possible for the women to be exposed to financial and sexual violence." "Psychologically," she added,

> sex workers experience high levels of Dissociative Identity Disorder. But, most importantly, prostitution is inherently a violent act because it shatters the basic principle of equality and tramples upon human dignity.

Representing the National Solidarity for Resolving the Prostitution Problem, Mi-rae Chung considered prostitution to be "a gendered violence." As such, she noted, it is important to approach the issue from a societal lens where, "like domestic or sexual violence ... it is a violence against women in our society."[29]

Conclusion

Thousands of miles from Seoul, Toni Van Pelt, the president of the National Organization for Women, spoke at a public hearing in Washington DC, unequivocally opposing a bill to decriminalize sex work. The argument was simple and direct: the bill would turn the city into a hotbed of sex tourism, relegate vulnerable women and girls into the trade, and sex work ultimately represents "the most extreme version of the violent oppression of women."[30] While this view had long been held by the leading feminists, such as Catherine McKinnon and Gloria Steinem, whose systemic and societal approaches to understanding gender inequality shaped much of the thinking around gendered violence in peripheral countries, there is a growing sense that an alternative explanation or position might be entertained and actually possible. The opposition group within NOW and the feminist circles in Korea question the foundational issues about survival, patriarchy, and choice. The leaders of local chapters of NOW are speaking out about the presumed contradiction between the right of women to choose what to

[28]In March 2016, the Constitutional Court, in a six-to-three-decision, rejected the challenge by a sex worker, Jeong-mi Kim, who sought to repeal the 2004 antiprostitution law, which criminalized voluntary prostitution. The Court supported the view of the feminist organizations that prostitution is inherently violative of human dignity. See, https://www.nytimes.com/2016/04/01/world/asia/south-korea-upholds-prostitution-ban.html. Accessed on March 11, 2020.

[29]See http://women21.or.kr/board_SWQx60/7577. Accessed on March 8, 2020.

[30]Retrieved from https://www.thedailybeast.com/the-national-organization-for-women-is-tearing-itself-apart-over-sex-work. Accessed on March 9, 2020.

do with their bodies as inviolable and the leadership position on prostitution as inherently violative of basic human dignity.[31] From a societal or global systems perspective, women relegated to commodified sex work, or international marriages for that matter, represents the perpetuation of patriarchy and the oppression of women. Others would argue that the act of telling the "prostituted women" what is best for them reconstitutes a patronizing and patriarchal thinking.

For now, in Korea, the leading feminist organizations successfully passed an Anti-Prostitution law that punishes the criminal wrongdoers and attempts to save the prostituted women from the immoral business of selling their bodies and transition them into a respectable employment. The ideological premise of this law, however, is not without some contradictions. In the article titled "Feminism and preventive act of prostitution: Can sex worker speak," Seong-sook Lee (2006, pp. 110–112) pointed out that the 2004 Revised Statute mimics social stratification produced through the patriarchal system. She noted:

> From early on, patriarchy generated a binary between decadent and virtuous women as a way of creating divisions … Perceiving sex workers based on the presumed superiority of the educated class position reifies the patriarchal-orientalist epistemology and eliminates the space for the subordinated subjects to speak for themselves.

Moreover, the feminists who support the prohibition of prostitution not only fail to dismantle the patriarchal system that discipline and surveille the women's bodies, but also ironically depend on the execution of the Anti-Prostitution law in the hands of the very symbol of patriarchal power, the Ministry of Justice, and the National Police. The power that rests with these organizations will not work toward the elimination of prostitution. Rather the prohibition of prostitution would only enlarge their power until the legal right to enforce the laws is eliminated. The striking resemblance in the way the dominant feminist organizations and advocacy leaders generate social discourse around marriage migrants and sex workers once again raises a difficult question: who has the power to advocate for whom?

[31]In their summary report to CEDAW regarding abortion, the Korean feminist organizations widely supported the women's right to choose. "Without having the rights for one's body," the report claimed, "women are again treated as tools for reproduction and mobilized for the nation's population policy" (CEDAW, 2010). This argument may be extended to the women's right to sell their bodies for survival, pleasure, or for any reason they so choose. The seeming contraction raises a question: Should the state or the leading feminist organizations dictate what is in the best interest of women?

Chapter 4

North Korean Defectors, *Koryoin*, and the Korean Chinese: The Ethnic Question and the Role of Advocacy Organizations

On September 7, 2019, a typhoon named "Lingling" (Liwayway) swept across the entire length of the Korean peninsula from the Jeju island to the North Korean capital city of Pyongyang, reaching beyond Southern Manchuria and causing severe flooding in the Russian Far East. The same day, a group of Korean Chinese gathered at the epicenter of Korea's public demonstration plaza in Kwanghwamun where 16-lane roadway encircles the statues of the Korean national heroes, General Yi Soon-shin and King Sejong, who imperiously exude confidence about the nation's proud past in the heart of Seoul. Despite the wind and the rain, some one hundred people showed up to the event in order to express their discontent with a North Korean defector who appeared numerously on a popular TV show, *Imahngahp* (acronym in Korean for Let Us Go Now and Meet), a variety show about the defectors' recalling of day-to-day life in the North and their adaptation experiences in the South. The defector in question had created and propagated a series of YouTube videos vilifying the ethnic character of Korean Chinese who encounter many North Koreans crossing the northern border into China. The event captures the complexity of a nation caught in the maelstrom of international politics and wars that propelled the Korean diaspora and forced people and the government to raise fundamental questions about "who is Korean?" and the accompanying rights, privileges, and responsibilities as Korean compatriots. Behind the struggles of diverse Koreans lies civil society organizations that not only advocate for their constituents but also reshape the contours of an ethnic boundary, challenge the essentialist notion of ethno-national belonging, and facilitate political engagements among differently marginalized Korean-heritage migrants in the South Korean context.

Organized Labor and Civil Society for Multiculturalism:
A Solidarity Success Story from South Korea, 69–90

Published under exclusive licence by Emerald Publishing Limited
doi:10.1108/978-1-83982-388-620200004

Korean Diaspora in Historical Context

Since the mid-1860s, Koreans in the northern region crossed the border into China and Russia, escaping economic hardship and the ravages of Japanese wars against China (1894–1895) and Russia (1904–1905), which eventually led to the occupation and colonization of Korea from 1910 to 1945. During this period, the Japanese military conscripted thousands of Koreans to work in mainland Japan, the Sakhalin Island in Russia, and the puppet state of Manchukuo in China. In 1919, the Korean independence movement leaders established the Provisional Government of the Republic of Korea in Shanghai in an attempt to invalidate the Japanese colonization of their native land and to resist against the colonial dominance through strategic military and diplomatic activities. When Japan invaded Manchuria (1931) leading to the Second Sino-Japanese War (1937), Soviet Union came to the aid of China and Stalin ordered all Koreans in the Russian Far East to relocate to the present-day Central Asia in Uzbekistan, Kazakhstan, and Kyrgyzstan.[1] The political realignment of Russia, China, and North Korea immediately after WWII and the emergence of communism in Northeast Asia contributed to the Korean War (1950–1953), which once again profoundly shaped the ethnic identity of Korean compatriots in these regions. In the aftermath of the Korean War, the military regime under general Park Chung-hee promoted emigration as a way of earning foreign currencies in order to aid in the country's economic development plans. Korean farmers traversed to various countries in South America, with Brazil serving as the most sought-after destination, where they worked on the government-funded agricultural lands but in just a few years transitioned into a niche economy in textiles. Koreans in South America represent an ethnic population that continues to dominate the industry today. During the same period, the cash-stricken government responded to West Germany's call for nurses and miners as guest workers, who were matched by highly educated students from North Korea to East Germany in order to study engineering and technical sciences. With the advent of the civil rights movement, the United States Congress passed a series of laws aimed at tearing down discriminatory social policies. One such law was the Immigration and Naturalization Act of 1965 that removed explicitly discriminatory provisions against select immigrant populations, including Koreans, other Asians, and Southern and Eastern Europeans. This law facilitated a massive emigration of Koreans to the United States, euphemistically called "*miguk*" or "the beautiful country." Over 2.5 million Korean immigrants and their descendants currently live in the Unites States, which represents the country with the most overseas Koreans, followed closely by China numbering about 2.46 million, Japan (825,000 Zainichi), Russia (170,000 Sakhalin Koreans), and Central Asia (500,000 Koryo-saram). In all, some 7.5 million Koreans and their offspring reside outside of Korea (Table 4.1).

[1]In the 1880s, Korea and Russia had established a series of overland commerce agreements and treaties allowing Koreans to cross the border and settle in cities like Vladivostok, Ussuriysk, and Pos'et (B. Kim, 2018).

Table 4.1. Overseas Koreans by Country, Select Years.

	2013	2015	2017	2019
China	2,573,928	2,585,993	2,548,030	2,461,386
USA	2,091,432	2,238,989	2,492,252	2,546,982
Japan	893,129	855,725	818,626	824,977
Canada	205,993	224,054	240,942	241,750
Russia	176,411	166,956	169,638	169,933
Uzbekistan	173,832	186,186	181,077	177,270
Australia	156,865	153,653	180,004	167,331
Kazakhstan	105,483	107,613	109,133	109,923
Vietnam	86,000	108,850	124,458	172,684
Brazil	49,511	50,418	51,531	48,281
Germany	33,774	39,047	40,170	44,864
Kyrgyzstan	18,403	18,709	19,035	18,515
UAE	9,728	10,356	10,852	10,930
South Africa	4,240	4,125	3,650	3,843
Other	434,188	434,198	441,290	494,918
Total	7,012,917	7,184,872	7,430,688	7,493,587

Source: Ministry of Foreign Affairs, Republic of Korea. "Status of Overseas Koreans," Various years.

Korean-Heritage Migrants in Korea

The rapid economic developments in South Korea coupled with highly visible international sporting events held in Seoul, such as the 1986 Asian Games and the 1988 Olympics, attracted the world's attention. Many Korean-heritage migrants from China, Russia, Central Asia, and North Korea began pouring into Seoul in order to take advantage of the expanding economic opportunities and the rising value of the Korean won (I. Yoon, 2005). The parallel political developments, such as the dissolution of the Union of Soviet Socialist Republics in 1989, leading to diplomatic ties with the Republic of Korea in the following year and with China two years later not only improved the social and political status of the heritage Koreans in these respective countries but also prompted a massive migration into Korea since the Japanese occupation and the outbreak of the Korean War.[2] In the process, the Korean government was forced to ponder

[2]The first meeting of the leaders between President Roh Tae Woo of the Republic of Korea and President Mikahil Gorbachev took place in Moscow on December 14, 1990, in order to discuss a wide range of issues governing bilateral relations. Two years

the meaning of "Koreanness" in the context of the rapid globalization in which Koreans were traveling and crossing national borders in unprecedented numbers.[3] How the Korean society today grapples with the question of ethnicity will significantly inform other important matters, such as multiculturalism, citizenship, and nationalism (Table 4.2).

Several important policy developments provided the legal frameworks for their entry, employment, long-term residency, permanent settlement, and citizenship acquisition. The Korean Chinese entered Korea in large numbers since the early phase of the Industrial Trainee System in the early 1990s. In fact, they constituted the single largest ethnic population among migrant workers in Korea. Some six years after the start of the guest worker program, a total of 206,461 migrant workers from mostly Asian countries toiled mostly in small- and mid-size factories.[4] The Korean Chinese numbered 32,260 or 15.6% of all migrant workers, but more importantly, 26,905 or 83.4% of them had overstayed their visas or left the factories and became unauthorized workers (JCMK, 2000). Recognizing the salience of globalizing economies and cultures, the National Assembly passed the Act on the Immigration and Legal Status of Overseas Koreans (hereafter Overseas Korean Act) on September 2, 1999. The law effectuated three months later, with the explicit intent of "lowering the barriers of national border to their motherland and strengthening each aspect of their daily lives." The Act significantly relaxed not only the immigration and residency requirements, but also laws pertaining to property acquisition, financial and foreign exchange transactions, medical insurance coverage, and distinguished services to national independence. Furthermore, the Act stipulated that it was the responsibility of the Government to provide "necessary support so that they may not be unfairly regulated or treated [relative to other Koreans] in the Republic of Korea." This Act would undergo 20 amendments since its first enforcement.

A few years after its passage, the Constitutional Court of Korea, however, decided that the 1999 Overseas Korean Act was "inconsistent with" the

---

later, on November 18–20, 1992, the new President Boris Yeltsin visited Seoul where the two leaders issued a joint statement in which President Yeltsin recalled the historic forced migration of ethnic Koreans from the Russian Far East to the Central Asian region and expressed that such acts and the subsequent repression of their rights were "condemned" in Russia. President Yeltsin also underscored the recent enactment of two laws, "Rehabilitation of Repressed Nationalities" and "Rehabilitation of Victims of Political Repression," would foster equal opportunities and restore political rights and freedom to the Russians of Korean origin. Retrieved from https://terms.naver.com/entry.nhn?docId=577316&cid=43860&categoryId=43862#TABLE_OF_CONTENT2.

[3]See the discussion of overseas Koreans who develop "competing notions homeland" (C. Song, 2014).

[4]The workers came from China, the Philippines, Bangladesh, Nepal, Pakistan, Thailand, Vietnam, Indonesia, Uzbekistan, Myanmar, Kazakhstan, Iran, Cambodia, and Sri Lanka

Table 4.2. Major Laws Impacting Korean-Heritage Migrants in Korea.

Industrial Trainee System	1991	Focused on companies invested overseas and, in 1993, expanded to domestic companies employing less than 300 workers (1+1)
Diplomatic Relations Established between Republic of Korea and USSR	1990	President Roh Tae Woo and President Mikhail Gorbachev signed the Declaration on General Principles of Relations between the Republic of Korea and the Union of Soviet Socialist Republics
Diplomatic Relations Established with China	1992	Prompted a massive immigration of Korean Chinese and ethnic Chinese as industrial trainees.
North Korean Refugees Protection and Settlement Support Act	1997	Minister of Unification is charged with developing a basic plan and a central office (named Hanaone) to aid in the protection and settlement of defectors.
Act on the Immigration and Legal Status of Overseas Koreans	1999	F-4 Visa: Defined "Overseas Koreans" Ministry of Foreign Affairs established the Overseas Koreans Foundation in order to foster overseas Korean networks, serve as Korean cultural resource, and identify talents among younger generations
Employment Management System	2002	F-1-4 Visa Special Employment Permit System allowed mostly Korean Chinese to be employed in the construction industry and seven other areas; the intent of this system was to reduce the number of unauthorized workers. Two years later, this system came under the Employment Permit System
Act on the Employment, etc. of Foreign Workers	2003	Introduced the Employment Permit System (E-9 Visa) in 2004, operating simultaneously with the Industrial Trainee System; the systems unified under EPS in 2007; employed initially for three years, but in 2009 the extension of two years was permitted
Immigration and Legal Status of Overseas Koreans – Revised	2003	Revised Overseas Korean Act that added pre-1948 emigrants and their descendants.
Visitation Employment System	2007	H-2 Visa: Eligible overseas Koreans from China and former Soviet Union countries over the age of 25 can be employed in 32 industries and sectors including the manufacturing, construction, and service.

Source: Compiled by the author from various sources.

Constitution's equal protection clause and prompted an amendment.[5] The Act had originally defined the "Overseas Koreans" as those individuals who left the country after 1948 since the establishment of the modern Korean republic shortly after its independence. Due to its temporal restriction, the Act only applied to post-1948 emigrants and effectively left out a host of Koreans who, for a variety of reasons, migrated earlier to neighboring countries to China, Russia, Japan, and Central Asia. Many of these emigrants had fought for Korea's national independence and were forcibly relocated to the present-day Central Asia.[6] To exclude them arbitrarily not only favored recent emigrants to countries like the United States and Canada but also contradicted the basic rationale of the law. Some 10 years later, the National Assembly enacted the Special Act to Support the Residency Acquisition of Koreans in the Former Soviet Union Countries (hereafter Koryoin Compatriot Act). This law further supports overseas Koreans by charging the Minister of Foreign Affairs and Trade with the responsibility to ensure that Koreans in affected countries do not remain stateless as many had not applied for citizenship in countries like Uzbekistan and Kazakhstan after the dissolution of Soviet Union that created the independent nation states. The main aim of the law was to fulfill the country's responsibility to protect the Koryoin by collaborating with the appropriate countries. Specifically, the law articulated the need to support them in gaining legitimate resident status in these countries, sustaining economic self-sufficiency, and fostering Korean heritage by establishing cultural centers through which they may continue to utilize the Korean language and gain access to information and technology (Koryoin Compatriot Act, 2010).

The laws concerning the treatment of North Korean defectors depart significantly from those governing other Korean-heritage migrants. To begin, the law titled Special Law to Support National Heroes and North Korean Returnees was enacted in April 1962 in order to elevate the status of North Korean defectors at the same level as those who fought for the Korean independence and/or otherwise demonstrated meritorious service to the nation. This law was amended in January 1979 providing compensation, followed by the North Korean Compatriot Returnee Protection Law in June 1993, a newly titled law to reflect the transition in their status from national heroes to recipients of basic livelihood programs. In 1997, the name changed once again to North Korean Refugees Protection and Settlement Support Act, charging the Minister of Unification with the responsibility to provide a wide range of support for their resettlement, such as education, employment, accommodation, medical care, minimum living standards, and financial resources. Aside from the major name changes, numerous amendments were passed in order to systemize the support resources.[7] Since its enactment, the

---

[5]Retrieved from https://casenote.kr/헌법재판소/99헌마494.

[6]Koreans in Russia and Former Soviet Union countries are called "*Koryoin*" or "*Koryo-saram*." The term "*Koryo*," from which Corea is derived, refers to the Koryo kingdom from 935 to 1392; *in* or *saram* means "person."

[7]The 2010 amendment established the North Korean Refugees Foundation and a preparatory school to facilitate their social integration; it also bolstered the employment support program. In 2012, the Foundation launched the "Employment

North Korean defectors increased steadily from 947 persons per annum in 1998 to its peak of 2,914 a decade later. As of December 2019, some 33,523 crossed multiple national borders in reaching South Korea. A significant trend since 2002 is that women constituted a clear majority, accounting for more than 80% of all defectors for the past 15 years (Table 4.3).

These foundational laws promulgated several employment- and residency-related programs and systems that guide the inflow of Korean-heritage migrants and their adaptation to life in Korea. In 2002, for instance, the Ministry of Labor launched the Special Employment Permit System (EPS), designed specifically to facilitate the employment of Korean Chinese, who had overstayed their visas and became unauthorized workers under the Industrial Trainee System, in the construction industry. Simultaneously, the Ministry of Justice established a new visa category (F-1-4), allowing Korean nationals to invite their overseas Korean relatives and granting employment opportunities in specific, service-related areas for two years. This system eventually came under the EPS – E-9 Visa in 2004. Three years later, the Ministry of Labor, in close coordination with the Ministry of Justice, implemented and managed the Visitation Employment System (H-2 Visa), which specifically targeted overseas Koreans from China and the former Soviet Union countries over the age of 25 and permitted employment in key sectors with significant labor shortage, such as the construction-, manufacturing-, and service-related jobs. Within a year, close to 300,000 H-2 visas were issued, and, for the next decade, the number remained steady. Similarly, the visas for F-4 (Korean heritage) dramatically increased from a mere 29,574 in 2006 to 444,880 in 2018 (Table 4.4). Consequently, the total number of Korean-heritage immigrants skyrocketed, with notable increases among the Korean-ethnic population from China, followed by equally significant increases among Koryoin from Uzbekistan, Kazakhstan, and Russia (Table 4.5).

Embedded Advocacy: The Politics of Ethnic Belonging

On the 54th anniversary of Korea's independence, some 30 Korean Chinese and Koryoin waged a hunger strike at the Myung-dong Catholic Church protesting the recent enactment of the Overseas Korean Act. This law applied the nationality principle of ethnic belonging and granted a wide range of privileges regarding employment, visitation, extended residence, business investments, and financial activities for anyone who was classified as "*dongpo*" (literally translated as "people who were born of the same mother" or compatriot). They protested the law's exclusion of individuals and descendants of migrants who left the country

---

Creation Program" and created a collaborative support network with the Ministry of Labor and the various industries; the Ministry also amplified and bolstered the North Korean Defector Integration Office in terms of budget and functions; additional changes were made in 2013 and 2014 focusing on providing capital development support, systemizing the three-year basic plan, and assessing the progress of the employment, education and other programs. Retrieved from https://www.unikorea.go.kr/unikorea/business/NKDefectorsPolicy/status/lately/

Table 4.3. North Korean Defectors Resident in South Korea.

	1998	2001	2004	2007	2010	2013	2016	2017	2018	2019 (Estimate)	Total
Male	831	565	626	573	591	369	302	188	168	202	9,363
Female	116	478	1,272	1,981	1,811	1,145	1,116	939	969	845	24,160
Total	947	1,043	1,898	2,554	2,402	1,514	1,418	1,127	1,137	1,047	33,523
% Female	12	46	67	78	75	76	79	83	85	81	72.1

Source: Ministry of Unification, Republic of Korea. 2019. "Number of North Korean Defectors Entering South Korea" (compiled by author).

Table 4.4. Korean-Heritage Residents in Korea by Visa Types, 2006–2018.

	2006	2008	2010	2012	2014	2016	2018
Total	267,436	421,155	477,029	538,277	704,536	775,715	878,665
Long-term residency (F-2)	35,746	35,688	32,205	13,374	11,791	10,867	10,488
Korean Heritage (F-4)	29,574	41,732	84,912	189,508	289,427	372,533	444,880
Permanent residency (F-5)	44	311	20,692	49,716	74,870	86,549	92,245
Work and visit (H-2)	0	299,332	286,586	238,765	282,670	254,950	250,381
Others	202,072	44,092	52,634	46,914	45,778	50,816	80,671

Source: Ministry of Justice, Korea Immigration Service (KIS). (2018a). "Combined Statistics of Immigration and Resident Foreigners," (compiled by author).
Notes: F-2, visas are issued to "persons married to Koreans." F-4, visas for Overseas Koreans as defined by the Overseas Korean Act; tied to the H-2 Visa type in that the eligible persons are permitted to work in fields that are determined to not cause labor market disruption; people over the age of 60 have been added. F-5, visas for people with special talents in the sciences, management, education, cultural arts, etc. as determined by the Ministry of Justice; former H-2 visa holders who have completed long-term employment in manufacturing, agri-dairy farms, and fisheries; former F-4 Visa holders who have lived in Korea for more than two years and fulfilled the minimum income and asset requirements; dongpo who are eligible to obtain Korean nationality through invitation by their Korean relatives. H-2 is a work visa issued to dongpos with family members in Korea; 3 years plus 22 months extension; permitted to work in unskilled labor occupations upon completion of employment education and application.

Table 4.5. Korean-Heritage Immigrants Resident in Korea.

	2014	**2015**	**2016**	**2017**	**2018**
China	606,964	647,717	652,028	702,932	728,539
USA	46,42	646,737	46,050	45,177	45,011
Uzbekistan	17,637	20,653	26,385	31,081	34,355
Russia	5,524	8,590	15,555	21,264	25,302
Canada	14,598	11,292	15,959	15,947	15,933
Kazakhstan	1,869	2,504	5,236	9,223	12,586
Australia	4,288	4,521	4,609	4,617	4,624
New Zealand	2,155	2,310	2,387	2,395	2,436
Other	5,075	5,998	7,506	8,672	9,879

Source: Ministry of Justice, Korea Immigration Service (KIS). (2018b). "Korean Heritage with Foreign Nationality" (compiled by author).

prior to the establishment of the Republic of Korea in 1948.[8] At the time of the law's passage in 1999, some 270,000 Korean Chinese and Koryoin out of 550,000 *dongpo* already resident in Korea felt betrayed by the Korean government's policy, which deliberately favored recent emigrants to the United States, Canada, and Australia since they constituted the majority of the post-1948 emigration.[9] As the protest continued for 10 more days, the leaders of the migrant advocacy organizations articulated and sought to restore a sense of "Koreanness" rooted not so much in common culture but by ancestry and blood ties. This sense of primordial ethnic identity represents one of several pillars of ethnic identification. The proliferation of Korean Chinese organizations not only supported the exponential increases in *dongpo* population but also played a key role in asserting their rights by firmly appealing to their homeland ties, with critical support from seasoned leaders of Korea's migrant advocacy organizations.

Shortly after ending the demonstration, the Reverend Kim Hae-sung,[10] who has been a leader among the advocates of migrant worker rights since the early

[8]Aside from this law, the Korean Chinese experiencing discrimination has significant impact on their mental health. See the article (Hong, 2018).

[9]Retrieved from http://www.0691.in/news_mail.html?no=58630. Accessed on April 10, 2020.

[10]The Reverend Kim graduated from Hanshin University where he actively participated in pro-democracy student protest movements. Upon graduation, he was introduced to a pastor in Sungnam who ministered to the poor and the homeless. Recognizing the importance of social outreach through ministry, he started a church for factory workers and opened a labor counseling office with the launch of the "telephone of hope." Foreign workers and Korean Chinese who had been employed in the Sungnam area solicited his help, and since then the Reverend has championed the labor and human

1990s, and three Korean Chinese, with support from two of the most well-known Korean civil society organizations, People's Solidarity for Participatory Democracy and Citizens' Coalition for Economic Justice (CCEJ), prepared and brought a suit to the Constitutional Court, claiming that the recently passed Overseas Korean Act had violated the Equal Protection Clause. Consisting of 61 civil society organizations, the newly formed consortium called "the Joint Taskforce Committee to Repeal Discriminatory Overseas Korean Act"[11] held a press conference urging the President to exercise his veto power. "Based on this law," the protesters claimed, "the overseas Korean society is divided arbitrarily between those who are legally defined as overseas Koreans and those who are not." "If the descendants of Koreans who migrated to China and Russia during and prior to the Japanese colonization are not considered overseas Koreans," they declared,

> then the venerable national independence leaders, such as the martyr Ahn Joong-geun who assassinated Ito Hirobumi, the first Japanese Resident-General of Korea, in Harbin, China or a celebrated national poet, Yoon Dong-ju, [who was born in Longjing, China, and died in a Japanese prison at the age of 28] are by implication not our *dongpo*.[12]

Two years later, the Constitutional Court rendered a decision that appealed to an ethno-nationalist sentiment reflected in the voices of the protesters rather than perhaps adhering to the letter of the law. The Court argued:

> this law on the surface uses a seemingly neutral criteria based on the principle of past citizenship as a basis to define the heritage Koreans [*dongpo*], however it intentionally excludes the Koreans from China and the former Soviet Union Republics whose ancestors have fought for the independence during Japanese occupation or migrated as forced labor.

"It is entirely unprecedented," the Chief Justice proclaimed,

> since no example exists from other countries where they would, rather than support, discriminate against their own countrymen who had to leave the country under the direst circumstances. It is

---

rights of migrant workers, serving as the founder and/or leader of, among many, Migrant Workers' House/Chinese Dongpo's House, the Joint Committee for Migrant Workers in Korea, and Korea Support center for Foreign Workers. He is touted as the "godfather of migrant workers" by some. Retrieved from http://news.unn.net/news/articleView.html?idxno=122670. Accessed on April 12, 2020.

[11]In Korean, the organization is called "*dongpochabyeol jeoedongpobeopahn cheolhoereul uihan gongdongdaechekuiwonhoe*" [동포차별 재외동포법안 철회를 위한 공동대책위원회].

[12]Retrieved from https://cafe.naver.com/russiainkorea/789. Accessed on April 10, 2020.

> further problematic to accept that the discriminatory nature of this law could be legitimized from a humanitarian, let alone a nationalist, vantage point. Thus, it would be difficult not to conclude that what this law attempts to accomplish through its discriminatory provision falls desperately short of overcoming the pain and division it would create among the heritage Koreans.[13]

In the end, the Court decided that the law was "inconsistent with the Constitution" and ordered appropriate and timely changes to the problematic section of the law.

While the Constitutional Court's decision marked a watershed moment for the heritage Koreans from China and former Soviet Union Republics, additional challenges still loomed large. For one, the Overseas Korean Act was not revised until 2004 and the Enforcement Decree was not made parallel with the revised law until 2007. Most importantly, the Overseas Korean Act only favored those with at least college education, wealthy investors, and high-skilled professionals while excluding low-skilled workers for a fear they would disrupt the domestic labor market (Lee & Chien, 2017). The government was also concerned about the rising number of unauthorized workers under the Industrial Trainee System and sought to stabilize the situation by introducing the EPS while enforcing stricter crackdowns and deportations. Disappointed and fearful, Korean Chinese and Koryoin, many of whom were at the time both unskilled and unauthorized, waged a hunger strike at Seoul Korean Chinese Church. On the 17th day of protest on December 29, 2003, President Roh Moo-hyun personally visited the church and expressed his firm resolve in front of some 2,800 protesters in supporting the right of *dongpo* to return to and live in their homeland. He commented: "Do not be discouraged by the law that inhibits your mobility across national borders, but be assured that the people are at your side."[14] In response, the pastor of the church, the Reverend Seo Kyung-seok, who founded CCEJ and served as its secretary general, gleefully ended the hunger strike. The following year, President Roh made it possible for the unskilled Korean Chinese to work in specified industries, eventually leading to the "Special Employment Permit System" (or Visitation Employment System) in 2007 where Korean Chinese and Koryoin would be permitted to enter and work in accordance with the Act on the Employment, etc. of Foreign Workers (hereafter Foreign Worker Employment Act).[15]

---

[13]The Court's opinion can be found here: https://casenote.kr/헌법재판소/99헌마494. Accessed April 11, 2020. The Court also pointed out that there is inconsistency in the way current laws conflict in terms of how each defines eligible "overseas Koreans." The Overseas Korean Foundation Act, which had passed two years prior to the Overseas Korean Act.

[14]The following article discusses the special relationship between President Roh and the members of the Seoul Korean Chinese Church. Retrieved from http://www.upkorea.net/news/articleView.html?idxno=17954#07Pk. Accessed on April 12, 2020.

[15]Moreover, the Ministry of Justice in June 2005 announced that Korean Chinese who

Despite these important changes, the Korean Chinese community continued to pressure the government to eliminate the remaining discriminatory provisions pertaining to heritage Koreans and to put into practice all aspects of the Overseas Korean Act, which ultimately would allow freedom of movement and employment. In commemorating the 20th anniversary of the Overseas Korean Act, a number of government representatives and overseas Korean organizations sponsored a forum titled "An Assessment of 20-Year Enforcement of Overseas Korean Act and the Challenge of Human Capital Development" in which Kwak Jae-seok, the director of Migrant Dongpo Policy Development Research Center, articulated a mixed message:

> The Overseas Korean Act is a good law. It allowed heritage Koreans in Korea and abroad to come together. However, the discriminatory provision of the Act still treats heritage Koreans as foreigners, and they have been reduced to social and political minority in Korean society.[16]

"Rather than treating heritage Koreans on the same level as Koreans," the Director continued,

> they were managed under the existing "Foreign Labor Policy" framework. Those who enter through the Visitation Residence (F-1-4) visa must register as foreigners, complete employment training, apply for a job through the employment support center, and finally sign the labor agreement.

Kim Jeong-ryong, the Director of Korean Chinese Social Problems Research Center, raised a more fundamental question, "are Korean Chinese *dongpo* or foreigners?" to which he asserted that "the government policies failed to fully embrace heritage Koreans." "The government must recognize," he continued, "that the Korean Chinese and Koreans share the same heritage, such that the familiarity with foods and customs make them 'cultural returnees' to their homeland."

---

entered Korea prior to the establishment of the formal diplomatic relations between the two countries in 1992 would be permitted to apply for nationality recovery, thereby normalizing their legal status. About 1,000 out of 5,000 Korean Chinese who had entered Korea prior to 1992 are eligible to recover the Korean nationality. Retrieved from https://news.naver.com/main/read.nhn?mode=LSD&mid=sec&sid1=100&oid=021&aid=0000110603. Accessed on April 14, 2020.

[16] "The 20th Year Anniversary of Overseas Korean Act … Experiencing Reverse Discrimination Instead." Retrieved from http://www.sbiztoday.kr/news/articleView.html?idxno=5747. Accessed April 13, 2020. Also, in the following article, Director Kwak assesses the effectiveness of the Visitation Employment System (H-2 visa). Retrieved from http://www.ekw.co.kr/detail.php?number=1510. Accessed on April 13, 2020.

Complementing the hunger strikes, legal battles, and public forums, the Korean Chinese and Koryoin communities demonstrated signs of proactively assimilating into the Korean society in diverse ways. This is all the more significant because they have been treated as an ethnic minority in China and the former Soviet Republics where numerous stories of mistreatment and legal discrimination abound. Their emotional embrace of Korea as their homeland bleeds into many areas of their political and social life. Two weeks prior to the national election in April 2017, the leaders of the various Korean Chinese organizations gathered at the steps of the National Assembly, holding signs in support of the presidential candidate, Moon Jae-in. Among them, the representatives of consortium organizations were present, including the National *Dongpo* Federation of Naturalized Citizens,[17] the Federation of Korean Chinese Associations, the Korean Chinese Women's Association, the Federation of Dongpo Nationals in Korea, and 12 other similar organizations representing the youth, teachers, artists, sports enthusiasts, merchants, and researchers.[18] Utilizing this opportunity to support a prominent political figure, the *dongpo* communities simultaneously issued the following three demands: (1) immediately repeal the restrictive *dongpo* residency policy and ensure freedom of employment in their homeland without being treated like foreigners; (2) enact a law to support naturalized *dongpo*s for the purposes of social integration and adaptation in their homeland; and (3) establish a national government office that can oversee all matters related to *dongpo* affairs, including immigration, social integration, and adaptation. Between 2014 and 2018 alone, some 53,988 persons acquired Korean citizenship, and of some 1 million *dongpo*s residents in Korea, about 20% (or 200,000), can vote in national elections. This trend is particularly significant in light of the fact that Korea has been struggling with a population decline due to the low fertility rate and Koreans acquiring foreign nationalities. In the same five years, the number of Koreans who renounced their Korean citizenship more than doubled those who became naturalized Korean citizens (Table 4.6). It is worth noting that, among the high-level government workers in foreign services, a total of 104 families acquired multiple

---

[17]In the 2018 national election of the Federation, the newly-elected President Cho Myung-kwon vowed to dedicate career in service of building and improving relations between Korea and China. Having served as the president of the *Korea Shinhwa Shinmun* (한국신화신문), he has years of experience relaying critical information and providing, among other services, legal counseling to Korean Chinese living in both countries. During the 17 years of residence in Korea, Dr Cho, who received a Ph.D. at Sichuan University in China, got married in Korea and has tirelessly sought to elevate the status of Korean Chinese. He always emphasized that "regardless of one's nationality, the Korean government will one day fully embrace Korean Chinese when they do their best and work hard." "Given that the total number of Korean dongpos has reached close to 1 million in Korea, the Korean Chinese are no longer foreigners but Korea is where their national roots belong." Retrieved from http://www.weeklypeople.co.kr/detail.php?number=3669&ckattempt=1. Accessed on April 14, 2020.

[18]Retrieved from https://blog.naver.com/sweethjj/221542368961. Accessed on April 14, 2020.

Table 4.6. Korean Nationality Recovery, Naturalization, Renunciation, and Loss.

	2014	2015	2016	2017	2018	Total
Naturalization	11,314	10,924	10,108	10,086	11,556	53,988
Recovery	2,886	2,610	2,303	2,775	2,698	13,272
Marriage – Korean naturalization	7,607	6,966	6,375	6,438	7,484	34,870
Renunciation	18,150	16,595	35,257	19,364	26,608	115,974
Loss	1,322	934	1,147	1,905	6,986	12,294

Source: Ministry of Justice, Korea Immigration Service (KIS). (2018c). "Korean Nationality Recovery, Naturalization, Renunciation, and Loss," (compiled by author).

citizenships between the years 2011 and 2019.[19] In the context of globalization and the rapidly changing status of nationalities by choice, the debate about who should count as Koreans remains unconcluded. Finally, despite the conflicting opinions regarding the Overseas Korean Act, the Overseas Koreans Foundation Act, enacted two years earlier in March 1997, designed to "contribute to overseas Koreans, preserving national ties and living as exemplary members in countries of residence," defines "overseas Koreans" as "persons who, regardless of their nationality, retain the Korean blood and reside and make a living in a foreign country" (Overseas Koreans Foundation Act, 1997).

In stark contrast to the Overseas Korean Act, the Korean government's treatment toward North Koreans varied considerably. To begin, established in April of 1962, the first law titled Special Law to Support National Heroes and North Korean Returnees regarded the North Korean defectors on the same level as individuals who have meritoriously served the nation and provided support for their social and economic integration and adaptation to life in the Republic of Korea. This law, amended in 1979, considered the people who crossed the 38th parallel as "brave returnee soldiers" and implemented much enhanced and systemized support programs. The law's title changed once more in June of 1993 reflecting, in part, the changes in the political landscape where the returnees were classified as "recipients of basic livelihood." Four years later, the current law titled North Korean Defector Protection and Settlement Support Act (hereafter Defector Protection and Support Act) focused on providing diverse support mechanisms in order to foster their financial independence and social adaptation. Despite these transformations, the Korean government has always considered the North Korean defectors as Korean nationals deserving of all the rights and privileges of South Korean citizens in addition to supporting their livelihood

[19]The Yonhap News reported that 83 out of the 104 families that have multiple citizenships haven chosen the United States nationality. Retrieved from https://www.yna.co.kr/view/AKR20191008156200001?input=1195m. Accessed April 14, 2020.

through numerous educational, employment, and social integration services. More importantly, the Article 3 of the Constitution of the Republic of Korea, established in 1948, stipulates that "the territory of the Republic of Korea shall consist of the Korean peninsula and its adjacent islands," effectively including all North Koreans as co-citizens. Furthermore, the Article 4 states "the Republic of Korea shall seek unification and shall formulate and carry out a policy of peaceful unification based on free and democratic order." One may reasonably infer from these two principles that, both geographically and politically, the South Korean people and the government embrace North Korea as their own and strive toward democratic unification.

Unlike their *dongpos* from China and former Soviet Union Republics, the North Korean defectors never had to struggle to become South Korean citizens.[20] Upon declaring their intention to defect to the South, all such North Koreans became eligible for citizenship and subject to protection under the existing laws. The process of integrating the defectors starts with the National Intelligence Service who conducts a necessary investigation in order to determine the types of protection and support individuals may require. The defector is then sent to a special center established through the 1997 Defector Protection and Support Act called Hana Won where they go through 400 hours over 12 weeks of social adaptation education, including psychological stabilization, learning about general life in the South, career counseling, and basic employment training. For the first five years, the government is also required by law to provide financial and other human capital support for their livelihood, such as school transfer issues and associated fees, employment support funds, housing, and personal protection. Article 30 of the Defector Protection and Support Act also mandated the establishment of the North Korean Defector Support Foundation under the tutelage of the Ministry of Unification.[21] In close connection with the Foundation, numerous civil society organizations operate some 25 social integration and support centers nationally, coupled with volunteer organizations providing integration assistance, professional counseling, and general services.[22]

---

[20]There are many other challenges, however. Chung (2008) documents ways in which North Korean defectors must negotiate their shifting identities between "defector" and "migrant" as well as overcome numerous barriers to their social integration in the South. Similar issues in the following Special Issue edited by Kim (2016) address the intersection of the government policies, the role of civil society, the media and the individual agency of North Koreans living in South Korea. Finally, Kim and Jang (2007) discuss the hardships, maladjustment issues and emotional isolation that reflect North Korean status and experience.

[21]Established on March 1, 1969, the Ministry of Unification has been charged with collecting public opinion and managing all matters concerning the unification issues in a systemic and institutional manner. The name of the foundation changed to Korea Hana Foundation in 2014. Here the word "*Hana*" means "one" or "together" in Korean.

[22]Retrieved from https://www.unikorea.go.kr/unikorea/business/NKDefectorsPolicy/status/entry/. Accessed on April 16, 2020.

From the vantage point of the Constitution and the government, the North Korean defectors can potentially play a significant role in bringing the two countries together. Not only does this special, historical purpose set them apart from perhaps other heritage Koreans, but also their painful experiences of having to leave behind their family members, who may be subject to harsh treatment or persecution, create tremendous psychological anxiety and trauma that other returnees with relatively greater freedom and choice could not possibly fathom. One may get a glimpse of their mental and emotional struggle for survival in the South as it is often powerfully and symbolically revealed through their urgent voices in and desperate appeals to international communities. An organization known as PSCORE (People for Successful Corean Reunification) was founded in 2006 by Kim Young-il, a defector-soldier who has dedicated his life in the South to address any barriers to unification, support fellow defectors adjust to life in the South, and advocate for human rights in the North. Having established a special consultative status with the UN Economic and Social Council since 2012, PSCORE has prodigiously participated in various Human Rights councils and commissions in order to bring awareness to the international communities and South Korean citizens.[23] Their work addresses the country's historical tragedy wrought by international geopolitics and brings to focus the important work of national unification through which they forge a unique sense of Koreanness rooted in history, blood ties, and shared aspirations.

In submitting its 2014 report to the United Nations Universal Periodic Review, PSCORE had conducted interviews with defectors who arrived in South Korea between 2005 and 2011. Their ages ranged from 26 to 55, and their experiences underscored "the prevalence of torture, public executions, forced labor, and death sentences for minor offenses." These "eye witness accounts," the report commented, "reveal that all 30 articles of the Universal Declaration of Human Rights are regularly violated and many of the DPRK's citizens are denied even basic rights." In all, some 120,000 political prisoners are detained in "total control camps," "where hunger and abuse are common, death rates are high" including children. The overall conditions in North Korea are simultaneously driving many to go abroad in order to find better opportunities for work and to improve the quality of life. In another report titled "North Korean Workers Overseas – State-Sponsored Slavery," PSCORE, however, documented the precarious conditions under which North Korean migrants work across 16 countries from Russia and China to Poland, Myanmar, and Ethiopia.[24] They are employed in a variety of manual labor industries, such as mining, logging, textiles, and construction, and earn wages dependent on how jobs were procured. The North Korean government charges an exorbitant monthly fee, which, in many cases, amounts to

[23]Moon (2014) argues that "South Korean human rights NGOs resumed active advocacy targeting the international community by exposing poor CPR (civil and political rights) situation in North Korea through transnational human rights networks."
[24]Other countries include Mongolia, Kuwait, United Arab Emirates, Qatar, Angola, Malaysia, Oman, Libya, Nigeria, Algeria, and Equatorial Guinea.

90% of the workers' wages. Pointing out numerous violations of international covenants,[25] this report asserts that not only do these workers labor long hours and have their wages withheld, but also they are strictly regulated and surveilled by North Korean officials often in collusion with the host states.

The cross-border migration between the neighboring countries of North Korea and China in modern times dates back to the early days of the 1950s. Largely motivated by an economic hardship-opportunity gap, Korean Chinese traversed to North Korea throughout the economic growth periods of the 1960s and 1970s. In fact, the North Korean government offered incentives for the Korean Chinese to work and live, including housing, food, work, and money.[26] The economic conditions between the two countries completely reversed in the 1990s as China emerged and would become an economic giant in the next two decades, while North Korea struggled to develop viable economies even to satisfy the basic necessities for the majority of its population. The changing economic and political landscape during this period prompted a reversal of migration between North Korea and China. It is estimated that some 50,000 North Koreans regularly cross the Tumen River into China where they often encounter and solicit assistance from the Korean Chinese.[27] Over the years, the Chinese government has flexibly regulated the North Korean defectors, allowing at times for the workers, who are paid significantly less than the Chinese workers, to fill labor demand, while in other times, it has tightened the enforcement and deported thousands of defectors.[28] Many North Korean women who cross the border and end up with

---

[25]These include: International Covenant on Economic, Social, and Cultural Rights, the International Covenant on Civil and Political Rights, United Nation's TIP Protocol (the Protocol to Prevent, Suppress, and Punish Trafficking in Persons, Especially Women and Children), the Convention against Torture and Other Cruel, Inhuman, and Degrading Punishment or Treatment (CAT), among others.

[26]Hazel Smith, a North Korean scholar, notes that "of the 28,028 persons discovered crossing the border into North Korea in 1961, over 7,000 stayed in North Korea." However, many attempted to cross the Yalu and Tumen rivers illegally and lost their lives. In an effort to stem the tide of illegal cross-border migrations, both countries entered an agreement in 1964. This Protocol stipulates that such migrants ought to be repatriated except in case of natural disasters. Retrieved from https://www.wilsoncenter.org/publication/explaining-north-korean-migration-to-china. Accessed on April 17, 2020.

[27]According to a Korean Chinese researcher from China's Social Sciences Center, it was estimated that some 4,800 North Korean defectors were repatriated to North Korea in 2002 alone. This number is more than twice the number of North Koreans who have defected to South Korea in the same year. The fate of these repatriated North Koreans has been well documented by the defector testimonies. Retrieved from https://news.naver.com/main/read.nhn?mode=LPOD&mid=tvh&oid=055&aid=0000100168. Accessed on April 17, 2020.

[28]The Chinese government expressed deep concerns about the possibility of spike in crime in the Korean Chinese community of Longjing, Jilin Province, because of the increased unauthorized migrants from North Korea. Written in both Korean and

Korean Chinese men oftentimes must leave their children behind in China when they get deported.[29] The preponderance of North Korean defectors in the Korean Chinese communities not only complicated the political relations between North Korea and China but also generated equally complex social conditions of dependence, abuse, and violence. In the border town of the Jilin Province, China, a Korean Chinese pastor, who has been actively supporting the North Korean defectors and conducting mission work in the area, was found dead, raising speculations that the North Korean government may be responsible.[30] The incredible stories of their challenges and resilience are being heard more and more as they finally make their way to the South.

The various heritage Koreans in the Northeast Asia are crossing paths in the most unusual and dire circumstances. In the context of economic destitution, social isolation, and political persecution, the migrants demonstrate tremendous courage and determination. Despite the complexities, the history of Koryoin who returned to their ancestors' homeland some 80 years after Stalin ordered the forced relocation is reinvigorating a nationalist sentiment that may facilitate a unified Korean identity or at least contribute toward its mosaic. As a first gathering of its kind, some 140 members of the National Network of Koryoin came together in Ansan, Kyunggido, and issued the "Koryoin Declaration," in which they affirmed the Korean identity and vowed to become a contributing member of the Korean society. With tears in their eyes and in the emotion-filled auditorium, the third and fourth generation Koryoin, who barely can speak the Korean language, recalled the names of the Korean national independence movement leaders and declared themselves proud descendants of these national heroes and honorable sons. "As the circumstances during the past 80 years caused the Koryoin to split into 15 different national groups and compelled us to lose our ancestral language," they remarked, "we have always held our ethnic tradition in high esteem and maintained our Koryoin identity." "We still hold in our hearts," they went on, "the spirit of our ancestors who remind us that, while we were born

---

Chinese, a banner warned the residents to "hand over your possessions and protect your life when foreigners [North Korean defectors] aggressively panhandle or attempt to take your personal belongings." Retrieved from https://news.naver.com/main/read.nhn?mode=LPOD&mid=tvh&oid=055&aid=0000467001. Accessed on April 17, 2020.

[29]As these incidents of North Koreans crossing into China, particularly the Yanbian region, increased rapidly since the 1990s, the government-run media in China empathetically treated these tragedies without doing much to support the women. The following report suggests that such a contradiction was exposed in the mainstream media may be indicative of changes within the Chinese government. Retrieved from http://news.tvchosun.com/site/data/html_dir/2014/10/22/2014102290096.html. Accessed on April 17, 2020.

[30]Retrieved from http://www.gomtv.com/view.gom?contentsid=14255674&auto=1. Accessed on April 17, 2020.

in another place, we live everyday remembering our ancestors' country."[31] "Our hope," they pleaded,

> is that the government of the Republic of Korea, the National Assembly, and Korean citizens help our Koryoin families integrate into the Korean society as we seek to live in harmony with our brothers and sisters, upholding the Constitution and respecting its histories and cultures.

In commemorating the 150th year of Korean migration to Russia, the advocacy organization called Peace Asia organized a drive rally across the Siberia-Korean Peninsula. Leaving the Ahn Junggeun Memorial Museum in Seoul's Namsahn Mountain, the motorcade consisting of Koreans and Koryoin drove through the Military Demarcation Line across the 38th parallel that was established by the armistice,[32] crossing the Eurasian continent and reaching finally in Moscow under the banner "Eurasia's Road of Peace, Peninsula's Road of Unification." Having served as a co-representative of the CCEJ, the recently inaugurated Director of Peace Asia, Kwon Oh-byung, commented, "a countless number of people have been pained by the divided Korea, but the overseas Koreans in this region have been doubly abandoned by both the North and South Koreas." "If we can transform our paradigm from war and confrontation to peace and reconciliation," Kwon added, "then I anticipate the role of our overseas Koreans would be expanded."[33] Echoing these sentiments, President Moon Jae-in, during his visits to Central Asia in April 2019, coordinated an informal meeting with Kazakhstan Koryoin whose ancestors have laid their lives or otherwise contributed significantly to preserving Korean heritage through Korean language, history, and cultural education. Addressing the crowded audience, President Moon conveyed his commitment with Kazakhstan and its neighbors in expanding opportunities for economic development and promoting peace in the region. Moreover, he expressed a plan to relocate the remains of two independence fighters who perished here in commemoration of the 100th anniversary of the March 1st movement. Finally, in fulfilling the spirit of our ancestors, President Moon urged the

---

[31]Retrieved from https://newsis.com/view/?id=NISX20170917_0000097764&cID=10803&pID=10800. Accessed on April 17, 2020.

[32]The armistice, which ceased hostilities between the two sides, was signed by the U.S. Lieutenant General William Harrison, Jr. representing the United Nations Command, and the North Korean General Nam Il for the North Korean and Chinese armies.

[33]As he was preparing to celebrate the 100th anniversary of the March 1st movement, the government announced that it would allow the fourth generation Koroyins to remain in Korea, as defined and protected under the Overseas Korean Act. Previously, the Act allowed only up to the third-generation descendants of the first generation of Korean migrants to former Soviet Union Republics. Retrieved from https://www.yna.co.kr/view/AKR20190212106900371?input=1195m. Accessed on April 17, 2020.

Koryoin to be of the same heart and mind in transforming the nation into a nation that embraces new ideas and promotes peace throughout the peninsula.[34]

Who Is Korean? The Ethnic Question and Heritage Koreans

On November 7, 2019, the President Moon Jae-in administration came under intense criticism by domestic and international human rights organizations when it decided to deport two North Korean defectors. These two seamen had boarded a ship and attempted to cross the Northern Limit Line, a maritime demarcation separating between North and South Koreas, after allegedly killing 16 other crew members. The human bloodstains were discovered on the ship. Within days, the administration decided to return the men back to the North through Panmunjeom, the building where the armistice was signed, acting on the belief that these shipmen had "committed a heinous crime, demonstrated psychological instability, and could potentially commit future crimes." Completely surprised and disappointed by the lack of care regarding the handling of this case, the Human Rights Watch's Phil Robertson issued a critical statement, expressing that "the South Korean government should have thoroughly investigated the charges and provided them with an opportunity to state their case against deportation." "Although it may be possible, as the South Korean government insisted, to not consider the two individuals as potential refugees," he continued, "the human rights laws and protocols to which South Korea is a signatory forbid deporting individuals to countries where they may be subject to torture, other types of brutal treatment or death." Adding to this observation, Yoon Yeo-sang, the director of the Database Center for North Korean Human Rights, pointed out that "any North Korean person who enters the territory of South Korea is automatically a South Korean citizen, and, upon expression of their intent, then at that point they become North Korean defectors." They further articulated that this heartless act was unprecedented particularly given President Moon's record as a human rights lawyer, and the government's rationale referencing the Defector Protection and Support Act was a complete misreading of the Act as it permits exclusion of certain individuals from receiving such support and protection but does not mention anything about deporting such individuals.[35]

A few weeks after the incident, Kim Hyun-chul, the Minister of Unification visited Washington D.C. on an official business and participated in informal discussions with Korean residents in the area. The event was sponsored by the D.C. chapter of the National Unification Advisory Council, which consists of over

---

[34]The two people whose remains will be returned to Korea and buried among the national heroes were Kye Bong-wu, who continued to advocate and taught Korean language and history during exile, and Hwang Wun-jung, who fought in the resistance army against the Japanese soldiers during the 1920s in the Russian Far East region. Retrieved from http://www.korea.kr/news/policyNewsView.do?newsId=148860228. Accessed on April 17, 2020.

[35]Retrieved from https://news.joins.com/article/23632112. Accessed on April 18, 2020.

3,600 members throughout the world in 124 countries. During the Minister's speech, an audience member unveiled a sign, which read, "the murderers of deported North Korean young men" and, written below it, the names of President Moon and the Minister Kim. Shortly after the protester was escorted outside the meeting hall, the event sponsor named Choi Min-seok disparaged the alleged misbehavior of the individual. It was later revealed that the protester was named Park Sang-hak, the leader of an organization called Fighters for Free North Korea and the Federation of North Korea Human Rights Organizations. During the heated exchange between the two men, Choi declared, "You came from North Korea? Is that something to be proud of? the North Koreans are not permitted to enter!" Adding to a barrage of insults, Choi spewed out in utter condescension, "How dare you claim to be a Korean citizen?" implying that no one considers him a proper citizen of the Republic of Korea. These insults reflect in part the manner in which the North Korean defectors are perceived and treated in South Korea. It is even more disturbing that such thoughts would be harbored and voiced by people who supposedly work toward the nation's unification. His comments reflect a major disconnect between South Korea's Constitution (and its attendant legal frameworks) and the general attitude toward North Korean defectors who experience tremendous difficulties adjusting to life in the South. The North Korean defectors are citizens by law, but significant challenges remain for them to be accepted and belong.

In a similar way, the Korean Chinese have struggled to integrate in Korean society and faced numerous challenges based on the popular perception regarding their perceived criminality and untrustworthy ethnic character. Such an essentialist notion about the Korean Chinese became a source of national attention when a group of some 43 Korean Chinese organizations, representing 660,000 Korean Chinese residents in Korea, protested the airing of the movie, *Midnight Runners*, where Daerim-dong in Seoul was depicted as a place full of "Chinese persons without proper documents who frequently engage in atrocious crimes, thus should be avoided at all costs."[36] One other scene showed a Korean Chinese person kidnaping runaway girls, forcing oophorectomy and selling the removed ovary in a black market. This is not the first time in which a popular movie painted the Korean Chinese community in such a light. Other movies, unfortunately abound: *The Yellow Sea* in which the Korean Chinese are shown to be closely connected with professional killers for hire; *New World* showed a character name "Yanbian beggar" who again played the role of a Korean Chinese professional killer; finally, the movie, *Chinatown*, a Korean Chinese character played an organized crime member who operated on insolvent debtors and sold their organs to recover the money.

To make matters worse, a recently defected North Korean young woman, who appeared frequently on a popular television show, ignited a storm of controversy when she released a series of YouTube videos slanderously ascribing the Korean Chinese men with stereotypical images. In response, a group of Korean Chinese

[36]Retrieved from https://blog.naver.com/ska21c/221866939289. Accessed on April 18, 2020.

and other Koreans waged a public protest. What was interesting about this event was that the most representative Korean Chinese organizations had been absent at the protest site. In fact, they issued a statement countering the protest.[37] It reads:

> Currently, there are many North Korean defectors who live in communities where the Korean Chinese are concentrated. The term "peaceful co-existence" applies to all people, including the Koreans, the Korean Chinese, the North Korean defectors, and all other population groups. It also applies to nonheritage-Korean migrants who share the same space. While unfortunate, this act was done by a single individual and does not reflect the entirety of the North Korean population .... This year is the 20th anniversary of the Overseas Korean Act. In its commemoration, we shall endeavor to assess how the Korean Chinese community in Korea has developed. Moreover, we shall solicit assistance from a broad spectrum of Korean society to engage in a systematic assessment of the relationship among the Korean Chinese, the North Koreans, the Koryoin, and the resident Koreans .... We have been notified that the typhoon is expected to land on the Korean peninsula and make its way up to China and Russia. Because this typhoon is sure to cause serious damages, the report mentioned that we should be well prepared.[38]

[37]These organizations include the Federation Overseas Koreans in Korea, the National Dongpo Federation of Naturalized Citizens, and 10 other organizations.

[38]Retrieved from http://ekw.co.kr/detail.php?number=1767&thread=22r01. Accessed on April 18, 2020.

Chapter 5

Internal Orientalism and Multicultural Acts: The Challenges of Multicultural Education in Korea*

Introduction

In the past decade, South Korea (hereafter Korea) has undergone a significant demographic change due to the influx of international migrants. The Korean Immigration Service (2016) reports that the number of both long- and short-term foreign residents in Korea dramatically increased from 747,467 in 2005 to 1.9 million (or about 3.8% of the total population) in 2015. In response, the Korean government and non-government organizations (NGOs) implemented social integration policies[1] being aimed at reducing cultural conflicts and promoting multiculturalism, broadly captured under the umbrella term, *damunhwa,*[2] which is explicitly translated as "multi-culture."

---

* This chapter is a reprint of the author's previously published work: Kim, J. K., V. Basile, J. Jaime-Diaz & R. Black. (2018). Internal Orientalism and multicultural acts: The challenges of multicultural education in Korea. *Multicultural Education Review, 10*(1), 3–17.

---

[1]Korea's social integration policies consist of efforts to culturally integrate the marriage migrants, most of whom come from the Southeast Asia, the Philippines, and China, who intermarried with Korean men in rural areas. The Korean government established more than 100 Multicultural Family Support Centers throughout the country to provide a variety of social services, educational opportunities for the brides and their mixed heritage children, and cultural integration programs (J. Kim, 2011).
[2]The term "multiculturalism" is used in varying contexts to describe both the conditions and criteria of particular social, economic, and political arrangements in a given nation-state. Classical works on the topic are vast, and we seek not to list them here. In the South Korean context, however, this term is often used synonymously with the Korean word, *damunhwa*, which means literally "multi-culture." Currently, there is no uniformly accepted definition of this term, since it is used widely by governments, nongovernment organizations, television shows, and school textbooks. However, the general understanding of this term may refer to any policies, programs, and perspectives that recognize and value the importance of living in harmony with people of diverse cultural backgrounds.

Organized Labor and Civil Society for Multiculturalism:
A Solidarity Success Story from South Korea, 91–105

doi:10.1108/978-1-83982-388-620200005

The increased visibility and salience of the positive messages of *damunhwa* in Korea, however, presents challenges for multicultural educators. For one, there has not been sufficient time for the concept to take root through cultural osmosis and reinforced through institutional and organizational mechanisms, such as laws and policies, thus many students exhibit only surface-level understanding or harbor ideas that actually serve to undermine the intentions. More importantly, while *damunhwa* projects in Korea are generally conceived as liberal efforts to foster communication and understanding among diverse cultures, multicultural educators themselves may not be cognizant of the unintended consequences of programs that are aimed at promoting the virtues of diversity.

In order to identify the analytical shortcomings embedded in various *damunhwa* projects, this chapter extends Edward Said's classical work on Orientalism by analyzing the various ways in which the co-presence of diverse cultures in a single nation-state may produce, rather than eliminate, new forms of cultural dominance. Titled *Internal Orientalism*, this chapter addresses how the seemingly benevolent acts toward minority populations, ironically, have the effect of naturalizing and replicating the conditions of inequality, embedded in binary ideas and instantiated through performatives. Moreover, utilizing a descriptive content analysis of Internet news stories with the Korean word *damunhwa* in the headlines, this essay provides a support for the claim that, even as the Korean society attempts to demonstrate an overwhelming sympathy toward migrant populations, doing so obliquely hardens the line between the citizen and ethnic minorities; renders weak subjectivity by identifying the "Other" as socially, economically and culturally "at-risk" or vulnerable populations; and creates social–psychological opportunities for the Korean society to extend its benevolent hand as the owners and provider of cultural and material resources, thus solidifying the paternalistic relationship.

Internal Orientalism and Multicultural Performative Acts[3]

Said (2003) referred to Orientalism as "a style of thought based upon ontological and epistemological divisions made between 'the Orient' and (most of the time) 'the Occident.'"[4] It entails three basic dimensions: (1) a multitude of endeavors that describe and reify the Orient; (2) these activities, thoughts, and discourses

[3]The term "multicultural performative acts" derived from Judith Butler's notion of "gender performatives" (Butler, 1988) where she viewed gender as a performance through which individuals reinforce the socially resonant meanings regarding gender roles and identity. Similarly, multicultural performatives encompass a wide range of individual and institutional acts or performances that reify the concept of *damunhwa* in the Korean context.

[4]By "ontology," it refers to what actually exists, thus the division between the Orient and the Occident can be understood in terms of the "objective" or real differences in language, customs, religion, and mores. The epistemological divisions denote the manner in which we come to know and understand these differences through socially and culturally ascribed meanings, thus these involve our valuation of these perceived differences.

naturalize the distinction based on a binary; which (3) simultaneously activates the conditions of domination through the mechanisms of social ascriptions and performatives. The efforts to describe the Orient include not only misrepresentations and selective portrayals but also a significant investment in the production of a wide body of epistemic knowledge in the arts, travels, politics, science, and literature. More importantly, the real significance of such endeavors lay in the simultaneous construction of its mirror image, Europe, through negation. The theory of negative self-identification captures this process well, as the dominant culture normatively defines itself by positioning the Other in a conceptual binary opposition such that the descriptions of the Orient as the primitive, backward, and heathenistic, then, requires the "rhetoric of high cultural humanism" (Said, 2003, p. 227) that can shed light on the dark races through the force of civilization. Rudyard Kipling's (1899) poem, *White Man's Burden*, exemplifies the mutually binding, binary relations between the colonized and the colonizer as embodied in the "cult of imperialism" (Kaplan & Pease, 1994).[5] This speaks to the concept of culture as ordinary and normal (Williams, 1989) whose dominance against the new or external other should be protected (Stolzenberg, 2002).

Building on this theoretical foundation, the concept of "internal Orientalism" refers to the condition and process of not only marginalizing and devaluing of minority cultures within a single nation-state but also enhancing the current hierarchical relationship between the minority and dominant cultures that naturalize the system of inequality. In the arena of multicultural education, internal Orientalism suggests that the society's effort to address the quandary of diversity often reproduces, rather than ameliorates, the conditions of inequality through the performatives of "doing" culture in various educational and social contexts.[6] While

---

[5]The first stanza of Kipling's poem, *The White Man's Burden*, captures this idea: "Take up the White Man's burden –; send forth the best ye breed –; Go bind your sons to exile to serve your captives' need; To wait in heavy harness, on fluttered folk and wild –; Your new-caught, sullen peoples, Half-devil and half-child." This famous line was a rallying cry for Americans to go abroad and serve the needs of the Filipino people the year after the Spanish-American War.

[6]By "conditions of inequality," we refer to both latent, or unconscious, and manifest, or explicit, forms of discrimination that is embedded in social and cultural structures. There is a long history of colorism in Korean society where dark-skinned persons are socially devalued due to the perception that they earn livelihood outside of an office environment, such as in rural communities. Also, historically, children of mixed ethnic or racial heritages, particularly those who have a dark complexion, with certain non-white features, are equally denigrated due to the history of race mixing with American soldiers who are stationed in Korea. This perception is also largely gendered because many of the women who bear children with US soldiers were perceived to have been involved in sex work, which adds another layer of social valuation that affects the children of such mixed marriages. Given this context, ethnic minorities, who are visibly dark or whose parent may be from economically less well-to-do countries, are subject to a variety of mistreatments and discrimination, such as bullying in schools, social ostracism, and employment discrimination.

there are many examples of what might be called an "incendiary racism" (Amin-Khan, 2012) that exhibits overt discrimination and hostility toward an out-group, most of the liberal democratic societies no longer permit such outlandish displays of xenophobia and hatred toward minorities. But, what is perhaps an even more insidious form of Orientalizing is a subtle and symbolic construction of values and norms through repetitive, routinized acts.[7]

An example of this paternal routinization comes in feminism. Judith Butler (1990) theorized the manner in which individuals enact social conventions through the performances of day-to-day activities, including speech, mannerisms, intersubjective interactions, gestures, and thoughts. Because these social rules are historically constructed, widely accepted, and currently practiced, they provide an implicit blueprint or script for how individuals ought to behave in particular action contexts. To the extent that these social conventions are deeply embedded in society and constitutive of subjectivity, it becomes difficult to imagine an identity independent of socially constructed cultural trappings. Our taken-for-granted identities in terms of gender, race, nationality, and religion, for instance, are largely premised on hegemonic ideas that we enact through the generic process of routinized acts, thus they become an organic and natural part of our habitus, serving to replicate and normalize historical hierarchies.

The politics of multiculturalism in Korea is no exception in that it, too, reflects an outgrowth of particular social formations. For instance, the Korean government and numerous NGOs established a multitude of support centers for marriage migrants and their children in order to assimilate them into the Korean society. From elementary schools to universities, multicultural curricula and programs also emerged in the context of promoting *damunhwa* across cultural spheres, including the media, local governments, and religious-based organizations. The diversity of multicultural performative acts, however, embodies hegemonic ideas that standardize normativity through discourses, politics, and symbols of culture.

Constructing Vulnerable Populations and a Philanthropic Society

As a heuristic method, this section examines the manner in which "multicultural families" are presented to the public by analyzing latest news articles in one of the more popular Internet search engines in Korea and identifies a distinct pattern in the way the word "*damunhwa*" or "multi-culture" makes the headlines (Table 5.1). Our main question concerns how the term, *damunhwa,* was used to promote programs, individual efforts, and government policies designed to address multifaceted issues surrounding diversity, diverse cultures, and diverse populations. We selected 50 most recent articles within the past year from the Korean-based Internet web

---

[7]Various sociologists expound upon the concepts of norm construction and routinized acts. Bourdieu's (1990) concept of habitus and Giddens' (1984) theory of structuration spoke to how individual acts simultaneously reproduce and create conditions for future action contexts, thus exhibiting and embodying structural qualities.

Table 5.1. Internet Search Results: Articles with the Word "Multi-culture" in the Heading.

1. Kangwonland Multicultural Children Language Diagnosis *Correction
2. Homeland Visitation Application Accepted for Multicultural Families in Iksan
3. TV Star, Joo Sang Wook of "Naejipi Natanatda," Meets with Multicultural Family … Makes their Dream Come True
4. Chinese Singer Hera – Politician Moon Jae-In Discuss Multicultural Policy at a Forum
5. KIC (Korean Investment Corporation), Unveils Medical Volunteer Plan for Multicultural Families
6. Let Us Work Together on Multicultural Program at a Library
7. Provides Cars-Gasoline-Travel Expenses to 14 Multicultural Families
8. Tutoring-Study Room Opens for Multicultural Families in the City of Kimchon
9. Multicultural Families Make Traditional Korean Chili Paste in the New City of Changnyung
10. Children's Library Launches "Together Happier Multiculturalism" Project
11. Accepts Application for Multicultural Families Wanting to Visit their Homeland
12. The Rainbow Choir Showcases "Multicultural Harmony"
13. Nonghyup (Agricultural Coop), Together with Multicultural Families
14. The Legend Baseball Zone Supports Lessons for Children of Multicultural Families in Jeju
15. Musical, "Ghost Friend," Addresses School Violence, Bullying, and Multicultural Themes
16. Enjoy Authentic International Dishes in Ansan's Specially-designated National Neighbourhoods
17. Politician, Lee Jae-Myung, Announces Locally-tailored Multicultural Support Programs
18. City of Sejong's Office of Education Offers Translation of School-Related Notices to Multicultural Families
19. Hope-Presents for Multicultural Families
20. National Assemblyman, Kim Myung-Yun, Hosts Multicultural-City Support-policy Forum
21. Multicultural Education-Counselling Centre-Village Projects in Progress
22. KBS (Korean Broadcasting System) – Home Countries of Multicultural Families Establish MOUs to Install TV Satellites
23. Project Supports Home Visitation for the International Women Marriage Migrants
24. Participants Requested for "Multi-Talent Program" for Multicultural Families
25. "Tong-Tong Our Family" – City of Kimje Multicultural Family Support Centre Launches Comprehensive Family Support Program in the Comfort of their Homes

Table 5.1. *(Continued)*

26. "Ladder of Love" Band, Hosts Global Multicultural Celebration
27. City of Ulsan Foreign Language High School – "Multicultural Day" to Promote Global Talent
28. Liberty Korea Party, City of Daejeon Women's Committee, Hosts "Making Traditional Korean Chili Paste" Event for Multicultural Families
29. Opening Celebration: Korean Language Classes for Multicultural Families
30. National Health Insurance Service Supports Home Upkeep Volunteer Work for Low-Income Multicultural Families
31. Opens Career Fair for Low-Income-Children of Multicultural Families
32. City of Ansan Multicultural Support Central Office, Recruiting Global Village Choir Members
33. Province of South Chonlla Office of Education <2017. Multicultural Family Experiential Learning Class> Opens
34. City Library of Kimje, Operates Multicultural Reading Program
35. Multicultural Education Counselling Centre, Experience the "Multicultural Village" at Suwon's Event
36. City of Inchon, Free Medical Exam for Multicultural Couples
37. "Multicultural Human Rights Lecture" for the County Employees at Gapyung
38. Full-Scale Study Plan: KAIST Professors, Multicultural Children
39. City of Asan Establishes "Multicultural Migrant Plus Centre" Opens in April
40. Agreement Reached with the City of Chilgok Community Health Multicultural Centre to Promote New Births
41. City of Jinan Police, Home Visitation Crime Prevention Classes – A Big Hit
42. County of Wanju, New Dance Class Opens, Healthy Family-Multicultural Support Centre
43. City of Iksan, "Home Visitation Classes to Promote Multicultural Understanding" Opens
44. Hanil University and Presbyterian Theological Seminary, Multicultural Family Mentoring Program Starts
45. Hana Multicultural Centre Darin "Producing Little Multicultural Lecturers"
46. Eradicate Domestic Violence among Multicultural Families
47. County of Kangjin, "Hope Cultural School" Opens … A New Array of Hope for Multicultural Women
48. Province of South Chonlla Office of Education, Multicultural Education Support Program Confirmed for This Year
49. City of Chuncheon New Village Support Committee, Delivers Scholarships to Multicultural Family Students
50. Multi-culture is "Our Neighbours-Friends-Family"

portal, http://www.naver.com, with the word *damunhwa* and eliminated duplicate news stories in order to capture the wide range of topics. This website is one of the top-five most used search engines in the world and has an unparalleled readership among the web surfers in Korea. Since all of the news stories were written entirely in Korean, the recognition of cultural subtleties in the way these programs are introduced to the public was equally important as the actual content. We subsequently analyzed each article and classified them into thematic categories based on the article's main context. A strong pattern emerged in terms of how the *damunhwa* projects painted the minority population as socially and economically vulnerable. We also identified subthemes based on economic and social vulnerabilities and language, education, and cultural deficits. In addition to these frames, *damunhwa* also invoked society's need to create cohesion out of diversity and implicated opportunities for experiencing, learning about, and helping the vulnerable populations (Table 5.2). Henry Miller (1969) referred to this as a form of "philanthropic colonialism" whereby the paternalistic assumption of cultural underdevelopment and the presumption of their social deficits coincide to create opportunities for intervention programs that construct an abstracted image of a benevolent society by exploiting "vulnerable" cultures as a commodified form.

In sum, the news stories overwhelmingly described *damunhwa* in one of two ways: (1) portraying multicultural families and individuals as either "at-risk" or members of culturally deficit populations or (2) showcasing benevolent acts and political opportunities for overcoming cultural conflicts of a diverse, philanthropic society.[8] The vulnerability language in the Internet news about multicultural families in Korea can be divided into two basic categories: at-risk and culturally deficit populations. When framing multicultural families as at-risk populations, the tone of the articles invariably reflected vulnerabilities based on social and economic disadvantages. Socially, multicultural families were perceived as particularly susceptible to domestic violence (see Table 5.1, article #46), which necessitated a "specially-tailored-service" (#17) and "home visits" by the police to prevent crime (#41). In one example, concerned about the rising cases of bullying in schools, a major theater company put on a musical to raise awareness about the "socially marginal," multicultural children (#15). These supposed social vulnerabilities are intimately tied to economic deprivations and disadvantages.

[8]A fine line separates between recognizing society's structural inequalities and ascribing social characteristics to a population based exclusively on the perception of frailty and weakness. The former calls into question the socially embedded structures and subtleties of power that produce conditions of inequalities, in terms of the distribution of wealth, access to pecuniary and educational opportunities, and social-psychological wages of tangible and intangible differences. The latter, however, socially stigmatizes the population by associating the community characteristics with intrinsic and inherent weaknesses and vulnerabilities, thus leading to social marginalization, a difference construction based on an inferiority–superiority binary, and an opportunity to do, ironically, philanthropic works on their behalf.

Table 5.2. Constructing Vulnerabilities Through the Use of the Word *Damunhwa* in an Internet Search Engine.

Vulnerabilities	**Programs**
At-risk/disadvantages	
Economically deprived	(2)(7)(11)(19)(23) Homeland visit support(22) KBS satellite TV service; (26) ladder of love – "warm aid"; (30) Home upkeep program
Economically disadvantaged	(5)(36) Free medical care; (31) career fair; (47) fashion design classes; (49) scholarship
Socially vulnerable	(15) Musical about multicultural children
	(17) Tailored support service
	(21) Programs for low-income multicultural family
	(41) Police home visitation crime prevention
	(46) Protect victims of domestic violence
Deficit/problems	
Language deficit	(1)(10)(18) Children; accent, language ability; translation service
Education deficit	(8)(29) home tutoring for parents
	(38) KAIST Professors serve as tutors
Cultural deficit	(9)(28) Making traditional chili-pepper paste; (24)(39) comprehensive support programs for the entire family
Commodification/opportunities	
Political opportunity	(3)(4)(17)(20) TV personalities and politicians show sympathy
	(14) Legend screen baseball
Promote social cohesion	(6) Multicultural reading
	(12) Rainbow choir; (32) global choir
	(13) Multicultural Women's College program; (48) Multicultural education
	(25) Communication and Social Integration program; (42) Dance classes; (43) Home visitation programs; (50) "Multi-culture is Us"
Experiencing cultures	(16) Designated neighborhoods as foreign cultural space; (33) cultural experience classes; (35) experience multicultural village
Globalization opportunities	(27) Promote global talent cultivation;
	(45) Training "little" multicultural educators
Combat low-fertility	(40) Childbirth promotion
Religious outreach	(44) Theological seminary sponsors one-to-one mentoring

Note: The numbers in parenthesis correspond to the Internet articles in Table 5.1 and Appendix.

Source: Compiled by the author.

The word *damunhwa* was often used in tandem with the phrase, "low-income," such that they were in need of basic services and gifts such as free medical care (#5; #36), career fair (#31), home upkeep support (#30), and "ladder of love" aids. Recently, one of the more popular programs financially supported "homeland visitation" for women who married into the Korean families. The Korean Broadcasting System (KBS), the largest and oldest broadcasting company in Korea, offered to install television satellite services in their homes, so that they may access television programs of their homeland.

The flipside of these seemingly culturally sensitive programs, however, was the generalized attitude about their intrinsic cultural deficit. Numerous multicultural family support networks and city government offices throughout Korea offered special language acquisition (#1) and improvement (#18) programs for children; other "home tutoring" programs for parents (#8; #29) facilitated their cultural assimilation. Even Korea's most prestigious professors and students from the Korea Advanced Institute of Science and Technology (KAIST, informally known as Korea's MIT) lent their support as one-on-one tutors for the children of multicultural families (#38). Moreover, in support of their cultural immersion into the Korean society, the international women were offered special lessons (#9; #28) on how to make the traditional Korean chilli–pepper paste, which incidentally is not commonly handmade in a typical Korean family's home but purchased in a marketplace. It is, thus, ironic that the multicultural women were expected to "compensate" their perceived lack of Korean cultural competency by becoming more traditional than the average Korean woman who may shriek at the idea of making anything traditional, such as kimchi, chili paste, or soy sauce, at home. The overriding idea behind many of these well-intended programs was that the cultural and language deficits among the multicultural families not only required comprehensive support programs for the entire family (#24; #39) but also established an ideological link to the population based on implicit notions about cultural shortcomings.

Defined as society's vulnerable populations, multicultural families become the subject to opportunistic programs that seek to elevate the social stature of individuals, politicians, and organizations. For instance, various politicians and television personalities (#3; #4; #17; #20) publicly show deep sympathy toward multicultural families and offer a multitude of special opportunities, such as a "name your wish" program, comprehensive service systems, and "legend screen baseball" outings. By extending this paternalistic hand in the public sphere, these politicians and television personalities elevate their own stature through commodification, while simultaneously reifying the cultural binary of the Other as "vulnerable" and "dependent."[9] Minority cultures also present the rest of the population to experience "difference" through "experiential classes" (#33), "multicultural villages" (#35), and neighborhoods designated as "foreign cultural spaces" (#16). Special outreach programs like the "childbirth promotion" (#40) for the multicultural

[9]This is also what the son of Warren Buffet called "conscience laundering" where those with means outweighing their needs "give back" (Buffet, 2013).

families and the church-sponsored mentoring programs (#44) present the host society with a wide range of new prospects that could turn cultures into a society's asset rather than a liability. These include new programs to cultivate "global talent" (#27), to train "little multicultural educators" (#45), and "global choir" groups dedicated to fostering communication and social integration.

Symbolic Orientalism: Noblesse Oblige and Eating the Other

The production of cultural binaries in societies with minority populations assumes many different forms and occurs often through the symbols of inferiority, marginality, and paternalism. In the absence of a concerted effort to understand and critique how race and ethnicity may deepen social inequalities, the cultural accounting of implicit and explicit differences valorizes the dominant cultural norm that can be activated in order to provide an ideological justification for discrimination and exclusion. Framed as oppositional dispositions, the seemingly progressive multicultural performative acts helping the less fortunate and experiencing minority cultures, foster instead the development of "relational epistemology" (Hirose & Phi, 2011) that both impacts various contact experiences and facilitates how the cultural Other is imagined.[10]

In April 2014, a Korean newspaper published a list of publicly elected officials who donated significant sums of money to help the less fortunate and the socially marginal populations. The organizations supported by these "noble" causes included the social welfare organizations, welfare institutions for persons with disabilities, a society for children with incurable diseases, and multicultural families. In the article, "Are These High-Level Public Officials Practicing Noblesse Oblige? Only 18 Officials Donated More Than $1,000 Per Year" (Ra, 2014), the news story featured the then Prime Minister, Chung Hong-won, who contributed more than 144 million won (US $140,000), while also citing a citizens' alliance group that revealed the list and lamented over the low number of contributors. Similarly, in promoting the culture of giving, the Social Welfare Community Chest established an exclusive club called the "Honour Society" for high-level contributors. Both of these examples are illustrations of "high cultural humanism" that supports the social class positions of the "noble" and the "dependent" Other. The "noblesse" high "Honour Society" must be made visible in contradistinction from the less fortunate members of the society. The binary construction of the interdependent relations, then, solidifies a power relationship, which is unbalanced due to the dominant position of one over the other.

Such an example of a binary construction resurfaces in different modes through implicit messages and symbols that reinforce the invisible but clearly apparent walls of cultural divisions. Numerous migrant advocacy organizations

[10]The phrase relational epistemology refers to the co-construction of the self and the other discursively through racialized Orientalist narrative, which suggests "the natural existence of categorical and essential differences between … the other and the self" (Hirose & Phi, 2011, p. 1487).

in Korea, for instance, demonstrate their support for diverse ethnic populations by hosting numerous cultural festivals. These cultural events prominently put on display the traditional attires and ethnic foods from many countries, such as Mongolia, the Philippines, China, Vietnam, Indonesia, and Thailand. However, this type of contact experience is both limited and surface deep, since there exist very little commonly shared cultural spaces outside of these special events. Flowers and Swan (2012) argued that these examples of "food pedagogy" of "official multiculturalism" were tantamount to "colonial food adventuring" where the dominant culture not only derived pleasure from "multicultural eating" but also achieved status distinction and cultural capital.[11] In doing so, the ethnic foods get reduced to "an object of appreciation by the cosmopolitan subject" who do not necessarily share their culture but deploy an "Orientalist narrative ... in the construction of a racialized and exoticized alterity" (Hirose & Phi, 2011, p. 1483). The outcome is predictably skewed in that the dominant and normative segment of the population experience the cultural Other, all in the name of humanism and cultural sensitivity that disguise the unequal structures of thought and interaction.

Borders of Race and Culture

The emergent ideas about cultural minorities and a myriad of multicultural performative acts in Korea simultaneously construct and reproduce visible and intangible markers of culture. The physical separation in the form of isolated ethnic communities compounds the symbolic barriers embodied in the politics of national belonging. These various forms of spatial marginalization exacerbate social distance whereby the dominant society cultivates the language of Otherness. In schools, workplaces, communities, and social spaces, the familiar trope about the ethnic Other naturalizes the habits of the heart and sustains the invisible walls of opportunity structures. The principal factor of segregation is intimately tied to the manner in which selected international migrants enter and become settlers in the Korean society. They include the guest workers through the government-sponsored Employment Permit System, the marriage migrants from Southeast Asia, China, and the Philippines, and the children of interethnic marriages. In each of these immigration flows, the international migrants and their children are already constructed ideologically as the culturally inferior Other, which makes their meaningful integration into the Korean society a challenging task.

In the City of Ansan, Kyunggi-do, a small township called Won-gok-dong is euphemistically named "a multicultural community without borders," which comprises more than 60 ethnicities. On the surface, it appears to be an exemplary

---

[11]Experiencing non-Korean cultures reflects a cosmopolitan lifestyle where an increasing number of Koreans now travel to diverse, overseas destinations, including Southeast Asia, the Philippines, Europe, and the Americas. For many who are unable to afford such excursions, the availability of multicultural festivals allows them to experience, albeit in a limited way, the seemingly middle-class sensibilities.

reflection of a multicultural society in transition. The community, however, is a symbol of both economic and cultural segregation constructed through the state-sponsored guest worker program that funneled young, predominantly male workers from overseas into an industrial city. As many scholars have noted (Choo, 2013; M. Kim, 2013; J. Kim, 2011) that Ansan's ethnic diversity is a direct outcome of the government's effort to control and manage temporary contract workers who were expected to return to their homeland after four-to-five years of employment in the city's predominantly industrial factories. Contrary to government expectation and design, the workers, many of whom overstayed visas, ended up settling their roots down in Korea. The Ministry of Justice, for instance, reported an increase of undocumented workers from 180,000 in 2005 to 210,000 in 2014 (Ministry of Justice, 2015). In order to support the increasing number of workers, ethnic enclaves of businesses, restaurants, and services proliferated within the past decade. The concentration of multiple ethnicities in a small geographical space is also often the subject of discursive rendering that casts the residents at best as the "necessary undesirables" and at worst as a cultural and criminal menace (Won, 2016).

In contrast to the foreign industrial workers, the so-called international marriage migrants experienced a fundamentally different reception from the Korean government and society. Responding to the shortage of marriageable Korean women in rural areas accompanying a massive internal migration from the countryside to cities, the local governments in Korea and privately run match-making companies aggressively campaigned to bring young women from China, Vietnam, the Philippines, Cambodia, and Thailand. As a result, the number of marriage migrants increased dramatically from 35,000 in 2005 to over 151,000 in 2015. In order to secure their long-term settlement in Korea, the government passed a series of laws that sought to structure the incorporation process of marriage migrants. The Multicultural Family Support Law in 2008, for instance, established over 100 multicultural family support centers throughout Korea and provided a path toward naturalization for marriage migrants (J. Kim, 2011). As of 2015, over 108,000 persons became naturalized citizens of Korea, an increase of more than 63% from 2010 (Ministry of Justice, 2016). Despite the seemingly liberal citizenship policy toward marriage migrants, the Korean government's uneven treatment toward diverse migrant populations came under intense scrutiny. In particular, feminist perspectives critiqued the constrained options under which migrant women attain citizenship in Korea. Framed as "ethnicized maternal citizenship," M. Kim (2013) observed that "the state projects emphasize marriage migrants' role as biological and cultural producers of "Koreans" while "relegating [them] as gendered dependents and ethnic others." Sponsoring a series of pre-migration "wife classes," the Korean government facilitated the institutional assimilation of marriage migrants, while prohibiting industrial workers from obtaining Korean citizenship. Because many of the women come from economically poor families with limited marketable skills, Korea's immigration and naturalization policies are "fraught with gendered meanings" including "the institutions of heterosexual marriage and family that offered material benefits, legal status, and moral inclusion in a community" (Choo, 2013, p. 464).

Among the children of interethnic marriages, they too must negotiate the borders[12] of race and culture as they strive to claim their rightful place in Korean society. Despite the admirable efforts of the government and NGOs in promoting multiculturalism in Korea, the children of mixed ethnic heritage continue to face obstacles and challenges. According to a report by the Ministry of Gender Equality and Family, the children of multicultural families under the age of 18 numbered 207,693, as of January 2015. Reflecting the sharp increase in interethnic marriages recently, the proportion of the multicultural children under the age of six constitutes more than 57% of the total, of whom some 38% are Vietnamese–Korean descent, followed by Chinese (19%), Korean-Chinese (13%), Filipino (9.4%), and Cambodia (5.5%) (Statistics Korea, 2014). These data demonstrate the increasing significance of multicultural children as they matriculate into and assume a larger presence in K-12 public school systems and become an integral part of the Korean cultural and social structures. Likewise, the negative consequences of difference, the Oriental Other, create, and expand disruptions. According to the National Human Rights Commission, a significant proportion of these children unfortunately experience bullying at school (37%), complain of accent discrimination (41.9%), and are told to "go back to your country" (21%) (Chosunilbo, January 2012), illustrating how students are enacting the effects of *internal Orientalism* in school settings.

Conclusion: Challenges of Multicultural Education in Korea

One of the major challenges of multicultural education in Korea concerns an understanding of the connection between social inequalities and educational content. Given the pervasiveness of social devaluation of non-western, minority cultures in Korea, multicultural educators bear perhaps the responsibility of providing quality educational outcomes for all students. This is an important responsibility that, however, needs to be shared with other sectors of the Korean society, such as the law, economy, politics, and culture.[13] Nonetheless, as an important dimension of multiculturalism, the field of multicultural education still could

[12]By "borders," we refer to both symbolic and physical boundaries that demarcate difference through performative acts and segregation of social, economic, and cultural spaces. The performative acts consist of a wide range of actions, both positive and negative, that reify cultural differences by ascribing social values to those differences. The construction of certain knowledge about particular ethnic groups also reinforce future action contexts that mediate social relations in workplaces, neighborhoods, and other public spaces.

[13]Multicultural education should not be perceived as the sole responsibility of educators, but it requires a concerted effort on the part of institutions and organizations that seek to promote and address inequity deriving from cultural conflicts and structural disadvantages. Thus, broadly defined, multicultural education involves the work of the various branches and levels of the government, the business, and the nongovernment sector.

play an important role in bridging the gap between multiculturalism as a rhetoric and reality.

Initially, Korea's multicultural education focused on ways to integrate children of multicultural families into Korean society by providing resources and support services for the students, parents, and families. Kim and Kim (2012), however, observed that, the majority of multicultural families reside in rural communities where multicultural education attempts were essentially assimilationist in scope. Others have pointed out that such efforts overlook how the Korean schools construct "othering of the targeted students as not-so-real or illegitimate Koreans" (Park & Watson, 2011, p. 3). This is largely because Korea's national curriculum explicitly emphasizes the country's "genetic and cultural homogeneity" (Park & Watson, 2011, p. 4) that is fundamentally at odds with the recent trend toward a pluralistic society. With an increasing focus on multicultural education, however, M. Kim (2013) added that the coverage of ethnic minorities is often limited to roles and topics related to racial issues such as discrimination. What is absent in the multicultural textbooks is how different minorities interact with each other and the social actions by ethnic minorities for social justice. Moreover, W. Hong (2010) articulated the critical need to reform teacher education programs in order to "produce culturally competent teachers" and to provide support for overcoming "significant structural barriers against minority groups" in Korea.

As a matter of priority, then, multicultural education in Korea should incorporate a critical approach. A critical multicultural education entails both teachers and students to look beyond their own lived experiences and their worldviews to enable them to understand the barriers that diverse groups confront (Howe & Lisi, 2017). Whether it is called "anti-racist practices,"[14] "critical race literacy pedagogy,"[15] or "social justice education,"[16] multicultural educators around the globe have in various ways addressed these shortcomings in both conceptualizing and delivering multicultural curriculum content. Hage (2016), for instance, identified six central functions of anti-racism, which may be used as a springboard for developing a network of active anti-racist pedagogy. These include: (1) reducing the incidence of racist practices, (2) fostering a non-racist culture, (3) supporting

[14]Aquino (2016, p. 105) argued that "institutional anti-racism challenges structural formations of racialized inequality" and extended the point further by stating that "everyday anti-racism … identifies the cultural repertoires that frame how individuals deal with racism across different contexts."

[15]Mosely (2010, p. 449) used the term "critical race literacy pedagogy" as a "subset of the approaches" of "multicultural education, culturally responsive teaching, and antiracist teaching" that "practice racial literacy in school settings."

[16]Lee and Walsh (2015, p. 45) suggested that, while the concept of "social justice education" is widely advocated to "address the educational inequities facing immigrant students," they point to the lack of adequate conceptualization and engagement. This concern, too, is particularly pertinent in the discussion about South Korea's multicultural education that attempts to mitigate not only the blatant forms of discrimination based on race and culture, but also how the mundane, everyday practices of differentiation contributes to social hierarchies.

the victims of racism, (4) empowering racialized subjects, (5) transforming racist relations into better relations, and (6) fostering an a-racist culture. Supporting these principles of anti-racism, Kohli (2008, pp. 181–182) argued that critical multicultural education should incorporate perspectives that "centralize race and racism," "other forms of oppression," "challenge dominant ideology," "represent a commitment to social justice," and "value lived experience." Paris (2012) furthered these ideas asserting that it is not enough for educational practices to respond to linguistic, racial, ethnic, and cultural changes in student populations, but that schools and teachers must seek to sustain linguistic, racial, ethnic, and cultural pluralism through meaningful educational pedagogies.

In the context of the Korean society, the concept of race or racism is not as deeply rooted in its history or cultural practices as much as the heightened state of colorism and xenophobia (Kim & Fu 2008; Rondilla & Spickard, 2007). Nonetheless, critical multiculturalism should first begin with the recognition that hegemonic ideas about culture and difference not only naturalize the reification of the Other but also shape their life opportunities in relational and, often, oppositional ways. Thus, Korea's dominant majority derives "cumulative gains" (Hage, 2016) in myriad ways by structurally and culturally marginalizing minority populations.

Moving beyond the emphasis simply on the "politics of mutual respect" (Hinderliter, 2009, p. 212), Korea's multicultural education also needs to reflexively challenge the ways in which a normative image of the good citizens vis-à-vis "good foreigners" gets constructed. As Hinderliter (2009) pointed out, culturally competent teachers must simultaneously examine how the perception of multicultural children as "foreigners in their own eyes" reify the binary opposition and shift the focus toward developing students who can both "navigate the dominant society" and become "active agents in challenging injustices" (Lee & Walsh, 2015, p. 63). To do so, each classroom addressing diversity can serve as a space of struggle where all students come to understand their particular location in relations to broader social issues, such as how immigration policies and economic stratification contribute to surveillance and racialization of distinct populations (Lee & Walsh, 2015). In short, just as racism and xenophobia necessitate resources, anti-racism also requires capacities to develop the "alter-politics confronting racism" (Hage, 2016, p. 132).

Chapter 6

From Labor Rights to Multicultural Human Rights: Migrant Advocacy Organizations and Praxis Multiculturalism

A day before the 54th Anniversary of the International Day for the Elimination of Racial Discrimination, the Joint Committee with Migrants in Korea (JCMK) held a press conference at the Korean Confederation of Trade Unions' building in Seoul under the heading, "No to Corona Racism." The panelists exposed the varied ways in which migrant workers fell through the cracks in the nation's effort to bring the spread of the Coronavirus Disease 19 under control despite the overwhelmingly positive assessment by the international community regarding Korea's systematic response to the crisis. The examples ranged widely from racist expressions and wrongful terminations to service denials in public facilities and government neglect.[1] Representing perhaps the last line of defense for migrant workers, the national umbrella organizations like JCMK have been relentless in their advocacy for migrants' labor and human rights. For over 25 years, Korea's migrant advocacy organizations unequivocally embraced the conundrum of addressing a myriad of labor and human rights concerns arising from discriminatory laws and treatments of non-Korean temporary workers. Despite the state's effort to reduce the impact and the reliance on international migrant workers, over two million migrants and their families now reside and work in Korea. The evolving demography of the Korean society generated attendant challenges of

[1]Because of the shortage of face masks, the government instituted a policy whereby only citizens and legal residents with a proof of medical insurance coverage were permitted to purchase. This left out tens of thousands of unauthorized migrants and temporary residents who could not apply for the nation's health insurance due to the six-month minimum residency requirement. Despite rave reviews of the Korean government's speedy and precise response to the virus outbreak, the migrant and ethnic minority communities in Korea experienced a sharp rise in discriminatory behaviors and xenophobic treatments. Retrieved from https://www.edaily.co.kr/news/read?newsId=03729366625705288&mediaCodeNo=257. Accessed on April 20, 2020.

Organized Labor and Civil Society for Multiculturalism:
A Solidarity Success Story from South Korea, 107–127

Published under exclusive licence by Emerald Publishing Limited
doi:10.1108/978-1-83982-388-620200006

working toward a one nation out of many ethnicities and races. Despite its relatively short history, Korea's unparalleled efforts under the heading of multiculturalism outpaced the society's capacity to address the diversity question and activated a mosaic of responses from the cross-section of Korean society. This chapter highlights the manner in which migrant advocacy organizations attempted to operationalize the language of multiculturalism in promoting the rights-based activism and maps out praxis-oriented principles and modes of multiculturalism.

Migrant Advocacy Organizations and the Multicultural Discourse

As the oldest and the most visible coordinating body, JCMK has been at the forefront of migrant advocacy organizations since its inception in 1995. The core leadership of the organization provided the ideological frameworks for migrant worker advocacy and the strategic guidance for organizing highly visible protests in response to the government's various labor importation schemes. In the early stage of its development, JCMK consisted of a diverse array of civil society leaders from religious and citizen groups to labor and pro-democracy movement organizations. Despite the wide spectrum of interests, the centrality of foci on expanding the labor and human rights of migrant workers and on providing counseling and legal services to migrant workers enabled the organization to grow quickly as the public discourse concomitantly started to tilt in their favor. The systemic flaws structurally embedded in the trainee system not only manufactured unauthorized workers but also exposed the vulnerabilities of migrant workers. As the news stories and television programs began to reveal the mistreatments toward migrant workers, the cross section of the Korea's civil society organizations empathized with these guest workers who simply demanded to be treated with civility, dignity, and fairly. The organizations' messages resonated powerfully with the public because of their moral high-ground position and the worsening precarity of the migrant worker condition. Consequently, the activation of the civil society organizations in support of JCMK's lead strengthened their political position and expanded the range of advocacy areas. Their success eventually led to measurable improvements, including the Supreme Court decisions regarding the recognition of trainees as workers, the payment of compensation to industrial accident victims, the application of Korea's labor standards law to all migrant workers irrespective of their legal status, and eventually the abolishment of the industrial trainee system.

The diversity of passionate voices within the organization generated fissures that led to the formation of a new umbrella organization. The main source of the contention centered on differences of approaches in addressing the core issues pertaining to migrants and the Korean society. However, the progressive religious leaders within JCMK focused on human rights–based advocacy, and the competing organizations viewed the labor issues as the dominant and fundamental areas of activism. In 2000, the new organization called the Migrant Worker Struggle Headquarter for Achieving Complete Labor Rights and Actualizing Freedom of Movement and Employment (MWSH) splintered from JCMK, and, in the following year, they helped to establish Seoul-Kyungin-Area Equality Labor Union, Migrant Worker Division, which would evolve into the Migrants' Trade Union (MTU) in 2005, fostering the working-class consciousness and supporting the autonomous, direct struggle by migrant workers (Y. Chung, 2014). Operating within the framework of the Korean Confederation of Trade Unions, MTU and its allied organizations sought to abolish the Industrial Trainee System and the Employment Permit System that gravely limited workers' fundamental rights of freedom to choose their employment and a chance at becoming permanent residents with five years of continuous employment and residence.

The MWSH member organizations' purpose and mission recognize the structural significance of migrant workers in Korean society and support their activism from a labor-focused lens. The Korean Contingent Workers' Center, for instance, articulates that

> the rise of contingent and irregular workers damages the foundational principle of "equal pay for equal work" and manufactures divisions within the labor ranks, thereby destabilizing the democratic order of labor-management relations. Such phenomenon also appears among the society's marginalized populations including women and minorities, thus leading to the deterioration of their quality of life and inhibiting their ability to assert their fundamental rights.[2]

The Labor Party also demonstrated its support for migrant workers, with the aim of "ending the capitalist exploitation of workers and striving towards emancipating labor through extinguishing the present-day capital-wage worker relationship."[3] Representing a host of citizen and labor organizations, the People's Solidarity for Social Progress "supports the establishment of labor unions and seeks to strengthen the unity and solidarity among the grassroots organizations in order to resist against the neoliberal globalization that perpetuates repression and violence against laborers, farmers, the underclass, and women." Other progressive organizations that struggle to bring about a more fundamental social change also joined MWSH, including the Marxian student organization called the National Student March, the Socialist Revolution Labor Party, the National Professor Association for Fair Democratic Society, the Public Interest Human Rights Law Foundation (Gonggam), and the Lawyers for a Democratic Society (MINBYUN). The scope of MWSH organizations that support the migrant worker rights reflects Korea's most progressive citizen and labor activists who have established an extensive track record in promoting democracy and labor rights.

---

[2]Retrieved from http://www.workingvoice.net/xe/index.php?mid=intro_center. Accessed on April 26, 2020.

[3]Retrieved from http://rp.jinbo.net/principle. Accessed on April 26, 2020.

Table 6.1. Migrant Advocacy Organizations.

	Labor Rights	Human Rights	Citizen Education	International Solidarity	Social Welfare	Social Integration	Multicultural Education
Joint Committee with Migrants in Korea							
1218ForAll	√	√	√	√	√	√	
Asan Migrant Workers Center	√	√		√		√	
Bucheon Migrant Worker Welfare Center					√		
Incheon Support Center for Foreign Workers	√	√			√	√	
WeFriends				√	√	√	√
Shalom House	√	√	√		√	√	
Paju Volunteer Center						√	
Pocheon House of Sharing						√	
Seoul Migrant Workers Center	√	√		√	√		
Asiansori (Asian Human Rights Cultural Solidarity)		√	√	√			
Suncheon Migrants Support Center						√	
Association for Foreign Workers' Human Rights	√	√			√		
Uijeongbu Exodus		√				√	
With Community		√				√	
Women Migrants Human Rights Center		√			√	√	
Won Buddhism Seoul Migrant Center					√	√	

Migrant Worker Struggle Headquarter for Achieving Complete Labor Rights and Actualizing Freedom of Movement and Employment						
Korean Federation Medical Activist Groups for Health Rights		√			√	
Kyunggi Migrant Joint Taskforce	√	√			√	
Public Interest Human Rights Law Foundation	√	√	√	√		
Imprisoned Laborer Support Committee	√	√				
The Labor Party	√	√				
Labor Social Science Research Center	√	√				
Labor Front	√	√		√		
Workers' Solidarity	√	√		√		
The Green Party	√	√		√		
Jogye Order of Korean Buddhism	√	√				
Cultural Action	√	√	√			
Lawyers for a Democratic Society	√	√	√	√		
Democratic Legal Studies Association	√	√				
National Professor Association for Fair Democratic Society		√	√			
Socialist Revolution Labor Party	√					
People's Solidarity for Social Progress	√	√		√		
Migrants' Trade Union	√	√		√		
Migrant Labor Hope Center	√	√				
Support Center for Migrant Worker Movement	√	√				
Migrant World TV	√	√	√			
Migrants Center Friend	√	√				√
Korean Confederation of Trade Unions	√	√		√		
National Solidarity for the Elimination of Irregular Labor	√	√				
National Poor People's Coalition	√	√				

Table 6.1. *(Continued)*

	Labor Rights	Human Rights	Citizen Education	International Solidarity	Social Welfare	Social Integration	Multicultural Education
National Alliance of Squatters and Evictees	√	√					
National Student March	√	√					
The Justice Party							
Earthians' Station	√	√					
Human Rights Committee of the Catholic Church	√	√	√				
Kasammako Filipino Union	√	√		√			
Association of Korean Buddhist Orders, Human Rights Committee	√	√					
Korean Contingent Workers' Center	√	√					
Solidarity for Migrant Human Rights							
Kyungsan Migrant Worker Support Center	√	√			√	√	
GyeongJu Migrant Labor Center	√	√					
Asia Chang	√	√				√	
Ulsan Migrant Center	√	√			√		
Solidarity with Migrants	√	√		√	√	√	√
Migrant Labor Human Rights Center	√	√					
Migrant and Human Rights Research Center	√	√			√	√	
Cheonan Moyse	√	√			√	√	
Korea Migrant Human Rights Center	√	√					

Source: The author compiled from the migrant center websites, where available.

Sharing some of the common areas of activism between JCMK and MWSH, the third leg of Korea's migrant advocacy umbrella organization is called the Solidarity for Migrant Human Rights (SMHR). The member organizations provide the basic counseling services to migrant workers, the marriage migrants, and multicultural families.[4] Some of the social integration programs include the Korean language classes, employment related trainings, and a variety of legal assistance programs as they relate to marriages, citizenship, and residency. The overlapping content of their mission is reflected well in Asia Chang (Window to Asia):

> we strive to create a society where all people share equally the basic rights and opportunities, transcending differences of nationality, skin color, religion, and gender. We further support a society that assures the inviolable dignity of each individual. Toward this end, we oppose acts of discrimination against migrant families based on differences of nationality and culture; instead, we aim to create a society that respects differences and fosters a community of friendship and harmony with migrants.

Other organizations share similar goals, articulating the uniqueness of each individual, the universality of humanity, the need to eliminate discriminatory behaviors, and the challenge of establishing a harmonious society that affirms diversity as a source of strength.

In many of the migrant advocacy organizations across the three representative consortiums, the notion of *damunhwa* (or multiculture) is loosely used to describe their programs and social conditions. While seemingly progressive in their overall messages, some of these "multicultural programs" reify cultural differences and reproduce cultural hierarchies by focusing on surface-level cultural artifacts and traditions. It is difficult to conceive that such programs designed to foster "multicultural human rights education" would yield a kind of society rooted in "peace, equality, and respect for human dignity." Rather than emphasizing programs that exoticize cultures through arbitrary experiential learning environments, perhaps alternative methods could be envisioned where diversity becomes a lived experience through strong and positive integrative designs that transcend classrooms or any particular programs. It is somewhat ironic to observe those organizations that seek to eliminate barriers to social and economic opportunities are perhaps already doing more for multiculturalism than many others with explicit messaging about its importance. Such a dilemma reflects the limitation of these advocacy organizations and presents important challenges at the moment and into the future.

---

[4]The topics associated with counseling services include unpaid wages, industrial accidents, workplace violence, human rights violations, immigration, free medical service, and other issues they face on a day-to-day basis.

First-order Multiculturalism: Intercultural Education and Cultural Democracy

The concepts of diversity and multiculturalism are very new ideas for most people in Korea. Understandably, the migrant labor advocacy practitioners seldom had any training or exposure to the concept until the government and the media began propagating it widely through promotion of various programs. Emphasizing "peaceful coexistence" with migrant populations, the concept of *damunhwa* has been loosely applied to a myriad of contexts where lofty principles of equality, human rights, and neighborly love abounded. From universities and government offices to corporations and civil society organizations, the concept is proving to be elusive as its goals are equally abstract and practically impossible to achieve. The complexity of issues surrounding the diversity conundrum is clearly very difficult to disentangle, but scholars have shed light on areas where attempts at achieving those goals failed and have provided a conceptual framework for establishing parameters to address its key aspects. Framed as the *first-order multiculturalism*, it describes attempts by the dominant society to reduce the gap between ideology of equality and the plurality of cultures (J. Kim, 2014). While enshrined in important national documents, the principle of creating unity out of diversity, under the first-order multiculturalism, outpaces the lived experiences of minoritized communities because of the preponderance of institutional, interpersonal, and systemic racism and discrimination. The persistent gap creates ideological dissonances and societal tension that may lead to greater instability and conflict.

In many countries of immigration, the diversity dilemma has a long history and continues to be a relevant, if not central, topic of discussion. While there have been significant improvements over time, many of these countries have faltered terribly in managing diversity. In the United States, for instance, the earlier efforts focused on the need to integrate minority populations in alignment with the majority's principles, values, and ways of life. The key motivating factor of *acculturation* schemes was a conflict reduction (Vickery & Cole, 1943), such that differences and estrangement of new groups required shedding of old cultures in place of a new American identity. Between the two World Wars, the ongoing global conflicts and domestic racial apartheid tasked the educators to develop productive *intercultural education* (Eckelberry, 1945). The abstract goals included ways to "correct the evils of intergroup bias and prejudice" (Kilpatrick, Stone, & Cole, 1949), "improve understandings and practices of good human relations" (Giles, Pitkin, & Ingram, 1946, p. 39), and "cultivate democratic human relations" (Taba & Van Til, 1945, p. 6). With an eye toward building a more harmonious and peaceful existence among diverse cultures, the intercultural educators sought to integrate newcomers under the banner of national unity. Several branches within intercultural education developed, with notable differences in approaches and methodologies. Consisting of mostly liberal white educators, the intercultural education premised on the idea that frequent interactions within a shared, common culture foster understanding and reduces differences of opinions and perceptions about each other. A great deal of emphasis was placed on personal responsibility to be good, non-discriminating citizens who embrace cultural difference with an open arm of tolerance, understanding and respect (Banks, 1993).

Although deviating somewhat from the minority cultural integration model of the acculturation and assimilation process, the *cultural democracy* model was introduced as a guiding principle for meeting the challenges of racially and ethnically diverse America (Davis-Du Bois, 1939). Strongly influenced by John Dewey's work on Democracy and Education (1916), the application of his theories to education in classrooms rested on the notion that "everyone has something to contribute" based on their experiences, but they must be simultaneously willing to uphold democratic values. Despite its novel idea, this experiment presented significant obstacles since it was difficult to address the notion of democratic education during the period in which social segregation, racial stigmatization, and economic stratification directly contradicted such lofty ideals. The gap between the principle of democracy and the actual lived experiences of minoritized communities was not easy to bridge. Similarly, the advocates of *cultural pluralism* predicated their arguments on the very notion that "the nation will be richer and finer in its make-up if... the country conserves the best that each group has brought" (Vickery & Cole, 1943, p. 31). Some were skeptical of the idea principally because of the possibility of creating cultural islands. Combining democracy and cultural pluralism, the notion of cultural democracy rested on three main tenets. First, all citizens must share a common set of beliefs, loyalties, and practices that promote democracy, not simply as a political idea but as lived experience. Second, individual merit and abilities are prized over group identifications or belonging. This is to enhance the notion that everyone has the equal chance at success, if each individual trusts the social and economic system to reward hard work and justly distribute opportunities for success. Third, people are free to exercise and practice their traditional cultures and faiths, but these customs must complement the core values of democracy. "When each individual has a respected place in a group," the theory suggests, "those native differences which might have been divisive prove instead to be of inestimable value in gaining a complete picture of a subject through the variety of points of view presented" (Hanlon & Diamond, 1945, p. 34).

These earlier efforts hardly produced the anticipated results. The lofty ideals of practicing democracy and extracting the best of cultures from diverse minority groups never really materialized. "The weed crop of social antagonism" continued to wreak havoc in society where intolerance, bigotry, and group hatred led to

> race riots, pogroms, masked riders ... as well as common varieties, including discrimination in employment, whispers at lunch tables, loose generalizations, social snobbery, mistrust, gentlemen's agreements on real-estate deals. (Taba & Van Til, 1945, p. 5)

After all, the challenge of bringing communities and schools together remained a dream deferred for a variety of complex factors. As one author aptly stated, "we learn what we live" (Kilpatrick et al., 1949, p. 568), but what was taught and how such lessons may have been communicated with students contradicted their lived experiences. As echoed by a prominent Swedish sociologist, Gunnar Myrdal (1944), what is quintessentially an American dilemma is the fact of dominant group's failure to recognize the persistence of inequalities and racism as their own making. "Our schools inculcate devotion to the American creed in theory," Brameld (1945, p. 94) noted, "but fail to give the minority groups equality and freedom in practice." "This inconsistency," Kilpatrick et al. (1949, p. 556) observed, "offends humanity at large ... and our intergroup discriminations condemn us before mankind." The irony was that blacks and other minoritized communities who experienced racism and discrimination on a daily basis must have relied on such lofty ideals of democracy, equality, and justice despite the repeated failures historically to fulfill their dreams of being treated equally and to be given a fair opportunity.[5] More importantly, the failure of intercultural education also stemmed from the false notion that conflict and hostility are primarily due to a lack of understanding. "Wars are fought between nations sharing the same cultural tradition," Hager (1956, p. 164) noted, "and the differences among allies have been greater than those between enemies." Referencing Myrdal, Hager continued, "the discrepancy between ideals and behavior cannot be adequately addressed by focusing on education, goodwill, and brotherhood because they avoid the head-on clash with community power structures." "The struggle for civil rights," he concluded, "falls victim to the philosophy of placation" (p. 165).

The Second-order Multiculturalism: Triumph of Civil Rights and Legal Protection

America's iconic poet, Langston Hughes released the poem titled, "Dream Deferred," in which he mused about what happens when one's dream never gets fulfilled. He asks, "does it dry up like a raisin in the sun? ... fester like a sore ... crust over like a syrupy sweet ... sag like a heavy load ... or does it explode?" This poem, written in 1951, perhaps foreshadowed the chain of events that would unfold across America and change the landscape of race relations for decades to come. From the Declaration of Independence to President Lincoln's Gettysburg Address, the notion of equality had always been an emblematic feature of an American society. Yet, both legally and through social convention, America's minoritized populations were relegated to the margins of society in nearly all aspects of their lives. Despite the earlier attempts to materialize the principle of equality, the civil rights movement of the 1950s and 1960s not only helped to breakdown legal barriers to equality but also inspired future generations to consider equality not simply as an emblem but as a social fact. The success of civil rights movement is difficult to quantify in measurable terms, but the enactment

[5]All of the major civil rights cases seeking to expand the principle of equal protection under the law have originated from contests waged by the minoritized communities who endured social marginalization in the form of discrimination, racism, and violence. These historical, legal precedents have impacted all Americans and considerably broadened the range of Constitutional protection for similarly marginalized communities.

of several key legislative decisions provides a framework for understanding the breadth of antidiscrimination efforts. The second-order multiculturalism describes a society where the beliefs and practice of sustaining equality are supported by legal rights and protection (J. Kim, 2014).

The 1964 Civil Rights Act served as the foundation for all other antidiscrimination laws. Complementing the Equal Protection Clause of the 14th Amendment, which prohibits unequal application and enforcement of laws to State's citizens, the Civil Rights Act has had a far-reaching impact on many areas of our lives, including employment, citizenship, voting, housing, and education. The law's prohibition of discrimination based on the race, color, religion, or national origin applied to the Age Discrimination in Employment Act of 1967, the Bilingual Education Act of 1968, and the Title IX of the Education Amendments of 1972 prohibiting sex discrimination in educational programs and federal financial assistance. Perhaps the most significant impact of the 1964 Civil Rights Act indirectly has been felt in the area of immigration and citizenship. The passage of the 1965 Immigration and Naturalization Act was a watershed moment, for it repealed a host of discriminatory immigration legal precedents against the Chinese (1882 Chinese Exclusion Act), Japanese (1907 Gentlemen's Agreement), South Asians (Immigration Act of 1917), Eastern Europeans (1924 National Origins Act), Filipinos (1934 Tydings-McDuffie Act), and Mexicans (Repatriation Act of 1935). Moreover, the new law replaced the anachronic Naturalization Act of 1790, which stipulated that only "free white persons" would be eligible for naturalized citizenship, thus permitting hitherto prohibited populations, mostly Asians, access to the prized American citizenship. The liberalization of immigration and naturalization policies fundamentally altered the ethnic and racial makeup of American society. More importantly, these measures represented a renewed commitment to equality and fairness, though additional challenges still remained beneath the surface.

Building on the successes of the historic 1954 Brown *v.* Board of Education and the antidiscriminatory provisions of the 1964 Civil Rights Act, the notion of equality began to pervade the educational institutions. Three major changes established a new path toward actualizing equality in the context of diversity that extended beyond race: the launching of the affirmative action policies in colleges, the establishment of ethnic studies as a discipline, and the federal mandate on bilingual education. Inspired by President John F. Kennedy's Executive Order 10925, focusing on taking "affirmative action" to ensure people are treated in accordance with the law, President Johnson in the following year delivered one of the most memorable speeches about the meaning of equality in the context of history. Addressing predominantly black graduates at Howard University, President Johnson stated:

> It is not enough just to open the gates of opportunity. All our citizens must have the ability to walk through those gates … We seek not just freedom but opportunity. We seek not just legal equality but human ability, not just equality as a right and a theory but equality as a fact and equality as a result (Public Papers, 1966, p. 637).

Shortly after his speech and as the student protests across the nation intensified, students of color began to occupy administrative buildings at San Francisco State University (SFSU) and the University of California, Berkeley (UCB) where, under the heading of the Third World Liberation Front, the students demanded a more robust representation of minorities through school curriculum and in the make-up of the student body, the staff, and the faculty. The establishment of ethnic studies departments at SFSU and UCB prompted the creation of hundreds of programs and departments intended to address the question of diversity and multiculturalism not only from the liberal white educators but also from the vantage point of minoritized communities. Finally, the sudden increases of Asian immigrants in the post-1965 period profoundly impacted not only the matriculation number of school-aged children in public schools but also the meaning of equal education as it relates to students who come from diverse cultures with limited English-speaking abilities. In a landmark US Supreme Court decision involving 13 Limited English Proficiency students, the Court argued that the students' inability to comprehend instruction in English violated the Civil Rights Act of 1964. The Court stipulated that "there was no equality of treatment even if students were provided with the same teachers, textbooks, curriculum, and facilities." The 1974 *Lau et al.* v. *Nichols* precedent established a new criterion for equal access in education for immigrant school children and, more importantly, mandated all K-12 public school systems receiving federal funds to develop bilingual education programs in compliance with the Civil Rights Act of 1964.

Paradox of Multiculturalism: Divergences of the Equality Discourse

One of the important successes of the civil rights movement is the placement of important liberal democratic principles of equality, justice, and fairness at the center of debates regarding multicultural education. From the right and the left of the political spectrum, scholars have vigorously and passionately articulated the reasons as to why the present-day multicultural programs are inadequate. Ironically, both groups defend and critique some aspects of the programs utilizing the shared language of equality. While the neoconservative political camp seeks to eliminate any program that fosters and solidifies group membership and identification, the liberal side is not entirely content with how the multicultural programs have evolved over the years. Regardless of the political positions, the most important impact of the civil rights movement and its attendant varieties of identity-based movements can be summed up by a neoconservative scholar who proclaimed that "we are all multiculturalists now," since "we all now accept a greater degree of attention to minorities and women and their role in American history and social studies and literature classes in school" (Glazer, 1997, p. 14).

From the conservative side, the recent adoption of laws to safeguard opportunities for minoritized populations was perceived to be a form of racial balancing. The main criticisms against various government and institutional programs, such as affirmative action and multicultural education, relied on two premises: (1) meritocracy and equality of opportunity prevail in our society; and (2) intentional and affirmative plans to promote diversity solidifies group identification and perpetuates "reverse discrimination."[6] While there were numerous ultraconservative intellectuals who opposed civil rights, some of the moderate conservatives raised important questions about the meaning of fairness as we struggled to implement specific programs to support multicultural endeavors. The first targeted area was the affirmative action programs at the university levels. In the first US Supreme Court decision, *Regents of the University of California* v. *Bakke*, the justices rendered a split decision where they invalidated a quota system based on the protected categories specified in the 1964 Civil Rights Act but upheld diversity as a "compelling state interest" requiring "strict scrutiny," thus allowing universities to take race as a plus factor in making admission decisions. Twenty-five years later, in 2003, the *Grutter* v. *Bollinger* U.S. Supreme Court case once again affirmed the earlier decision and articulated the "critical mass" argument that overcomes minorities being used in tokenized ways to legitimize institutional diversity. The conservative camp viewed affirmative action and other related efforts to promote diversity as violative of the core principle of equality. Steele (1997), for instance, viewed affirmative action as a form of "social engineering," allowing Whites to feel "a new racial innocence" in order to arbitrarily achieve proportionate representation (J. Kim, 2005, p. 12). Regarding multicultural programs, Arthur Schlesinger, Jr, in his book, *The Disuniting of America*, unequivocally critiqued the political nature of identity politics, claiming that "the cult of ethnicity exaggerates differences, intensifies resentments, and antagonisms, and drives ever deeper the awful wedges between races and nationalities."[7]

Among the liberal scholars, they too agree with the conservative viewpoint that the present-day multicultural curricular or programs are problematic. They contend that the current efforts do not go far enough to address the power structures but merely reflect "strategies of containment and co-optation" (Davis, 1996, p. 40). "Multiculturalism," Davis observed, "can become a polite and euphemistic way of affirming persisting, unequal power relationships by representing them as equal differences." Others have pointed out that multicultural education has been inappropriately conceptualized as "therapy, as a set of teaching techniques, or an academic discourse" (Sleeter, 1996). What is lacking is the "effective link with any broader movement for social justice … and to local struggles for power and

[6]Nathan Glazer's (1975) *Affirmative Discrimination* served as an amicus brief in support of Bakke in the 1978 case. Glazer and other neoconservative scholars have popularized the term "reverse discrimination," demonstrating the thinking that the history of racial discrimination has little or no relevance for the present condition and that it is largely up to individual's ability and willingness to seize opportunities rather than to be treated favorably because of one's race. Although very powerful and persuasive argument for some, it has the effect of reifying racial hierarchy because of the presumption of superiority–inferiority along racial lines, legitimizing antagonism toward minority populations and drawing focus on race exclusively at the expense of neglecting other myriad of factors impacting admissions or hiring decisions.

[7]Quoted in J. Kim (2014, p. 406).

voice" (Sleeter, 1996). "Antiracism," Gilroy (1990) contended, "is dependent on the delivery of justice and equity." Many antiracist praxis-oriented multicultural educators not only critique "trivialization or Disneyfying of cultural difference" and the "hierarchy that produces disparities in life chances" but also construct "effective classroom strategies to combat discrimination" and incorporate "engaged learning for democracy and justice." As the gap between what students learn in schools and the social need for multicultural education persists, multiculturalism that promote cultural, political, and social equality, as well as itself rooted in "a human rights-based movement," can be a transformative response rather a problem to be solved (Kymlicka, 2010). Finally, while multiculturalism is still very much a work in progress and significant gaps across the various milieus persist, it is worth noting that racism is no longer an acceptable social value in the public sphere for it fundamentally "transformed how we think and talk about race, shaping our actions as well as our beliefs" (Pitcher, 2009).

In order to overcome the ideological divide between the two political camps, it may be instructive to identify the exact source of contention and areas where they might both agree. The fact that both camps rely on the equality argument rather than some other opposing values is a promising starting point. The conservatives object to the liberals' use of the past examples of race discrimination to explain the present condition, accentuate racial divisions, downplay individual responsibility and merit, rationalize victim mentality, and reproduce reverse discrimination. The liberals critique the conservatives' failure to recognize the preponderance of racist attitudes in contemporary society, the systemic nature of discrimination and racism, the importance of minority experiences and contributions, and the role of institutions in rectifying social ills. The points of compromise may mean giving credence to both institutional and individual factors. More broadly, the multicultural dilemma reveals society's inability to strike the right balance between universal values and particular experiences, thus "recreating the stigma and inequality" (Olneck, 2011, p. 679) when we respond to difference or ignore it on account of equal treatment. The failure to reconcile the unity–diversity paradox also suggests that "the politics of multiculturalism characterizes a conflict inherent to social formations in which racism is simultaneously rejected and reproduced" (Pitcher, 2009, p. 456).

The Third-order Multiculturalism: Converging Diversity Toward Substantive Equality

The third-order multiculturalism highlights the necessity for moving beyond the language of equality to an active promotion of substantive equality by addressing inequalities that are embedded in institutions and structures. Consequently, the goal is to reduce the gap between the structure of opportunity and results, so that there exists natural and seamless representation of diverse groups. Most importantly, the integration of diversity is no longer something to be achieved through programs but reflects the state of heightened and positive consciousness whereby multiculturalism is routinized and normalized in everyday life. This requires fundamental changes in how we embrace multiculturalism, one that moves away from a mere program or validation of difference, as demonstrated through cultural festivals and other forms where culture functions as a fetish, to addressing structural and systemic forms of inequality and opportunity. Beyond the goal of trying to understand cultures and tolerate each other, social change through critical multiculturalism promotes multicultural interactions in all facets of social, economic, and cultural life. The third-order multiculturalism embodies shared spaces and resources, while reproducing relationships and structures that are natural and organic with significant reduction in gaps across ethnic and racial groups. Such patterning of thought and behavior embodies the new normal within the third-order multiculturalism (Table 6.2).

In already globalized societies, multiculturalism is no longer simply an outcome for which various stakeholders struggle to achieve but simultaneously serves as a mechanism for addressing potential conflicts. Multiculturalism is much broader than merely the co-presence of people from diverse cultures, but it signifies a substantively integrated society in all spheres of influence. The third-order multiculturalism, thus, signifies a strong integration of cultures in the context of promoting equality in key areas of civic and political life. Chart 6.1 illustrates the complexity of structures that impact the outcome and the medium of multiculturalism. The key factors and conceptual frames constituting the domains of multicultural praxis include the setting, spheres, and fields. The setting refers to the symbolic, material, and physical habitus where institutions, social relations, and power dynamics develop and operate.[8] Stratified societies that exhibit significant gaps between classes tend to have much stronger centralized ruling elite who control and dominate the subordinated classes and shape their worldviews. Based on the perspective of cultural hegemony, the dominant members of society collectively establish a system of control through which they reify ethnic group markers and foster the development of group identities.[9] Racism, thus, operates against individualism and instead cultivates group consciousness where intricate and detailed differences become magnified and socially valued. Thus, as Blumer (1958, p. 3) correctly observed

> race prejudice exists basically in a sense of group position rather than in a set of feelings which members of one racial group have toward the members of another racial group.

In a society where racism is a daily occurrence and pervasive, it would be counterproductive to emphasize individual effort to combat group-based biases and

[8]Using Bourdieu's definition, "habitus" signifies "structured structures predisposed to function as structuring structures, that is, as principles which generate and organize practices and representations" without rationally producing the intended outcome or expressly mastering the mechanisms for attaining particular ends.

[9]The concept of racialization applies here as it refers to the process of ascribing significance to difference based on immutable characteristics. Race-based classifications and cultural interpretation of divisions over time create distinct classes of people that become socially accepted and naturalized.

Table 6.2. Principles, Modes, and Orders of Multiculturalism.

First-order Multiculturalism	
Principles	1. Separation of races and ethnicities
	2. Equality as an abstraction: separate but equal
	3. Acculturation of newcomers: dominant group normativity
Modes	1. Legally sanctioned racial and ethnic segregation
	2. Ethnic ghettos and economic marginalization
	3. Prevalence of discrimination: antilocution, avoidance, structural discrimination, and violence
	4. Segmented and stratified labor market along racial and ethnic lines
	5. Wide social distance: psychological, physical, social, cultural barriers, and divisions
Second-order Multiculturalism	
Principles	1. Equality based on legal protection and rights
	2. Narrowing of social distance by removing structural barriers
	3. Affirmation of minority group experience and identity
Modes	1. Assimilation of newcomers
	2. Removal of legal barriers to equality in education, employment, housing, marriage, and other areas
	3. Proliferation of ethnic enclaves
	4. Social integration policies through affirmative action and other group-based programs
	5. Attempts at forced integration of schools, curricular, employment, and residence
Third-order multiculturalism	
Principles	1. Paradigm shift: multiculturalism as the new norm, not as a program
	2. Beyond the group rights discourse: return to individual rights
	3. Limited gap between equality of opportunity and equality of results
Modes	1. Seamless multicultural interactions in all areas of social, economic, and political life
	2. Elevated and positive consciousness regarding diversity and multiculturalism
	3. Proportional representation of diverse groups in all areas of public life
	4. Significant improvements of ethnic and class integration
	5. Reduction of gaps and social distance across ethnic and racial groups

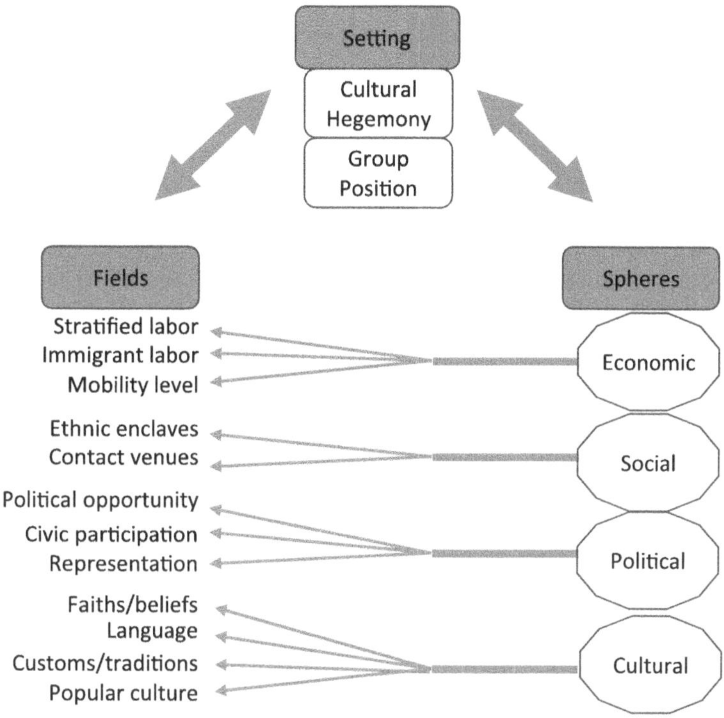

Chart 6.1. Domains of Multicultural Praxis.

discriminatory behaviors. Uplifting the status of socially stigmatized populations is important in minimizing conflicts and establishing a level playing field. A tangible goal of an ethnically and racially stratified society is to monitor the factors that contribute to the rigidification of boundary markers between groups and to ensure social equality of group positions.

The hegemonic controls of minority populations occur through the four main spheres of influence: economic, social, political, and cultural. Each of these spheres implicates fields where specific conditions of interaction contexts develop. Within the economic sphere, for instance, the dominant group permits the importation of ethnic populations who are seldom treated on the same level as the dominant population but pushes the newcomers to the very margins of society. The context for majority–minority interaction has been already predetermined by the existing superstructure through which the immigrant or other imported labor help to support an ethnically and racially stratified labor structure where there exist limited opportunities for upward or, in some cases, lateral mobility.[10]

[10]Various guest-worker programs historically have limited both vertical and lateral mobilities, including the US' Bracero Program, Germany's *Gastarbeiterprogramm* (Guest Worker Program) or Korea's *Goyong heogaje* (Employment Permit System).

When immigrant workers from particular ethnic or racial backgrounds are paid the lowest and relegated to socially undesirable occupations, the social stigma linking ethnicity and occupation deleteriously impacts their group position. The social sphere identifies the formation of ethnic communities, enclaves, and ghettos that serve as a symbolic marker for difference and for reciprocally justifying their economic marginalization. In order to narrow the social distance, these ethnically identifiable communities should demonstrate economic and cultural vibrancy, while fostering easy accessibility for the public. Other social contact points may be differentiated by ethnic markers, including the schools, places of worship, recreation venues, leisure activities, and intimate spaces.[11] The social distance between groups manifests through routinized activities already embodying significance of difference, thus the challenge is not to erase difference but to normalize diversity through habitual encounters. The main idea is to break down the invisible wall of culture without obliterating its authenticity and importance.[12] The political sphere accounts for the development of political opportunity structures where members of minority groups and their advocacy organizations may utilize culturally situated legal and ethical arguments, as well as rely on supranational measures and guidelines, in order to articulate counter ideologies and challenge the laws perceived to be discriminatory. The extent to which minority populations participate in civic engagements and their representation in politics may be indicative of the relative political openness, the organizational strengths of minority and its allied communities, and the culture of political participation in a given society. Minority participation in politics and policy changes reflects their integration into the host country. The extent to which a nation-state adjusts in law to protect the rights of minorities demonstrates its political openness and the possibility of greater minority participation. They are no longer guests or temporary sojourners but constitute invaluable members of a society. The cultural sphere exemplifies values, perspectives, and customs that individuals acquire in the course of one's life. For some, religious dominance occurs when members

[11]Sociologist Emory Bogardus developed the social distance scale in order to measure the level of intimacy between racial and ethnic groups. The scale was borne out of the tumultuous period of the 1920s in the United States where it was marked by the vitriolic antiimmigrant sentiments, the Eugenics movement, and the prevalence of racial violence and conflict (Wark & Galliher, 2007). The series of questions tested the extent of acceptance from the most intimate to least intimate associations one may develop with members of another group. The narrowing of the social distance circles included questions like, are you willing to accept a person (from a particular ethnic or racial group) as family, personal friends, neighbors on the same street, co-workers, co-citizens, noncitizen visitors, or exclude them from the country.

[12]"Given a population of ordinary people, with a normal degree of prejudice," Allport (1954, p. 281) concluded, "prejudice ... may be reduced by equal status contract between majority and minority groups in the pursuit of common goals. The effect is greatly enhanced if this contact is sanctioned by institutional support (i.e., by law, custom or local atmosphere), and it is of a sort that leads to the perception of common interests and common humanity between members of the two groups."

of a minority group practice faiths believed to be incompatible with the dominant members. Similarly, customs emanating from long and deeply held traditions may cause conflict and cultural dissonance between the groups. The fact that there are different traditions and faiths co-existing in one place does not necessarily lead to "clash of civilizations," but what matters is the degree of fluidity and acceptance of various traditions as guaranteed by the political system and practiced through a shared openness. As the interlocutor of a diverse society, the mainstream media not only communicates what may be newsworthy but also ascribes meanings to difference that can shape public's perceptions and emotive responses. Other cultural markers include foods, music, dance, clothes, and languages that could be made more accessible to the public without turning them into a fetish. Popular culture could also play a significant role in bridging the perceptible differences and lower the guard people have about each other's presumptions, sensibilities, and affective predispositions.

Korea's Migrant Advocacy Organizations and Praxis Multiculturalism

All multicultural societies have inevitably pondered ways to fulfill the motto, *e pluribus unum*, which signifies "out of many, one." The challenge of creating a unified society consistent with the core values of liberal societies demands intentional efforts in creating structures and habits of interaction where multicultural practices become normalized. Critical multiculturalism scholars invariably point out that "genuine multicultural education challenges hegemonic practices," and, in building a cohesive civic community, "support for diversity occurs within a framework of social justice and political equality" (Olneck, 2011, p. 679). A central dilemma of multicultural education, however, is doing multiculturalism without accentuating difference as it can unintentionally create stigma. The irony is that multiculturalists inevitably count race in order to overcome racism, whether it be through affirmative action, bilingual education, minority heritage celebrations, and a host of special programs recognizing contributions and uniqueness of "cultural other" groups in society where they are viewed and treated as marginalized population. There is no one who has more distaste for being treated differently, even seemingly positive and affirming ways, than the minoritized populations. We might call this *affirmative minoritization*. The extent to which societies grapple with cultural differences suggests that most people acquire meaning in things and experiences through a parochial lens. Approaches to multiculturalism perhaps require us to move beyond the provincialism of education in classrooms to real-life situations where the praxis of multiculturalism can be brought to life.

There are many things that are remarkable about Korea's migrant advocacy organizations in terms of their contribution to *praxis multiculturalism*.[13] From the

[13]Praxis multiculturalism refers to the conjoining of the conceptual issues regarding multiculturalism with lived practices. Rather than focusing on educating students and the public through multicultural celebrations and diversity trainings, praxis multiculturalism calls for putting into practice values of importance in multiculturalism.

very beginning of the industrial trainee system, JCMK mustered support from a cross-section of Korea's civil society organizations. Their message was simple and direct: It is morally reprehensible to mistreat international migrant workers. This message resonated through religious and citizenship organizations to labor groups and various professional societies such as legal aid consortiums, medical mutual aid networks, and social welfare entities. Not only did they rely on support from domestic groups but they also formed important ties with reputable international agencies such as the United Nations Commission on Human Rights, the International Labor Organization, the International Organization for Migration, and the Migrant Forum in Asia through which they adopted the language of equality and rights emanating from international standards, protocols, and instruments. The global approach stressed the importance of treating people with human dignity, something that is intrinsic to all human beings. The focus was not treating society's marginal populations favorably than the rest of the population but asserting their right to restore respect and dignity that has been taken from them through exploitive practices based on shortsighted economic systems and sanctioned through laws.

Because of the obvious precarity of migrants, the migrant advocacy organizations converged on rectifying the structure of inequality through changes in their labor and legal status. The government's position of using temporary foreign labor as a way to meet labor demand in 3-Ds (dirty, dangerous, and difficult) occupations exposed its shortsightedness. As numerous scholars have pointed out, the so-called labor-rotation scheme was designed to minimize social costs and maximize economic utility of young and able-bodied workers who are eager to satisfy the capital's demand. Its failure stemmed from the fact that the migrants are not machines but people with needs just like everyone else. The unintended consequences of temporary migration programs included, first and foremost, such programs seldom remain "temporary" because the host society develops dependence on labor that has become socially devalued. The reliance on ethnically and racially distinct labor and its associated social stigmatization leads to labor market stratification and isolation from which domestic workers increasingly shun. Ironically, the harsher the labor exploits and human rights violations, the more it is difficult for the migrants to return home since it takes that much longer for them to save from their earnings and, in that time, they will acquire externalities while living in a host country. The second important consequence in the Korean context is the activation of civil society. The formation of JCMK, SMHR, and MWSH is remarkable in terms of their unparalleled commitment toward labor justice, their many years of organizing protests against the government and capital aggressions, and the support they harnessed through legislative changes and public persuasion. They seek to accomplish this by addressing structural inequalities as seen through the perspective of various types of labor, including women, contingent, and migrant workers. Their refusal to be placated by minor concessions of the government and the business represents a beacon of hope for transforming the society toward multicultural praxis. Finally, the temporary migration programs ushered in other types of migrants who collectively are changing the demographic landscape of the Korean society. From marriage migrants and sex workers to Korean heritage migrants and refugees, the process and the movement in the making of a multicultural society has been initiated. While many of the government-approved and the civil society organization–sponsored programs to support, advocate for, and integrate migrants into the Korean society are laudable and unprecedented, building a cohesive society out of diverse populations requires still efforts that go beyond the rights-based approach.

When multicultural advocates speak of structural and systemic forms of inequality, one must bear in mind that, even as practices reflect good intentions, there is always a danger of reproducing the tendencies of cultural hegemony. In ethnically and economically stratified societies or in caste-like systems, the ruling elite maintains an intricate system of advantages and disadvantages that are controlled ideologically and embedded culturally. The notion of *noblesse oblige* captures the idea well in that the society's elite reinforce their superior social positionality through their acts of generosity and philanthropy. Such acts of kindness generate symbols of associations and structure a habitus for future relations. It is as if the masses of society's marginalized populations ought to feel grateful toward the nobility class' generous gesture by handing down their excesses. The patronizing acts and attitudes reinforce the relationship built on hierarchy and inequality. Unfortunately, these examples abound even among those who advocate for multiculturalism. In building a more robust multicultural society, Kymlick (2010, p. 137), a renowned scholar of multiculturalism, noted that "multiculturalism is first and foremost about developing new models of democratic citizenship, grounded in human rights ideals, to replace earlier uncivil and undemocratic relations of hierarchy and exclusion." Such a model, Kymlicka suggests, overcomes "the deeply entrenched inequalities that have persisted after the abolition of formal discrimination." The path toward an integrated society will certainly take time and tremendous effort. It will likely take more than just modeling a democratic citizenship, but co-constructing routinized interaction contexts where multicultural praxis may take root. Ironically, this means returning to the emphasis on individualism, not the kind that stresses individual freedom and isolation, but compassionate individualism where the needs of individuals are justly met and the burdens of communities responsibly shared.

Appendix

Website Addresses of the Articles in Table 5.1 (all articles accessed on March 13, 2017).

1. http://www.kwnews.co.kr/nview.asp?s=201&aid=217030300056
2. http://www.domin.co.kr/news/articleView.html?idxno=1143280
3. http://www.kookje.co.kr/news2011/asp/newsbody.asp?code=0500&key=20170304.99002000526
4. http://www.ksilbo.co.kr/news/articleView.html?idxno=581709
5. http://www.mt.co.kr/view/mtview.php?type=1&no=2017030611190846991&outlink=1
6. http://www.naeil.com/news_view/?id_art=229670
7. http://www.edaily.co.kr/news/NewsRead.edy?SCD=JC41&newsid=04670726615862008&DCD=A00304&OutLnkChk=Y
8. http://www.bzeronews.com/news/articleView.html?idxno=219455
9. http://www.hkbs.co.kr/?m=bbs&bid=local1&uid=419073
10. http://www.ajunews.com/view/20170310103233251
11. http://www.hkbs.co.kr/?m=bbs&bid=local1&uid=419073
12. http://www.asiatoday.co.kr/view.php?key=20170310010006292
13. http://www.rwn.co.kr/news/articleView.html?idxno=39340
14. http://www.newstomato.com/ReadNews.aspx?no=737584
15. http://www.focus.kr/view.php?key=2017031000102642560
16. http://www.incheonilbo.com/?mod=news&act=articleView&idxno=754510
17. http://www.fnnews.com/news/201703090917371894
18. http://www.ajunews.com/view/20170309123209394
19. http://www.ccdailynews.com/news/articleView.html?idxno=914294
20. http://www.incheonilbo.com/?mod=news&act=articleView&idxno=754820
21. http://www.joongboo.com/?mod=news&act=articleView&idxno=1150811
22. http://www.ksmnews.co.kr/default/index_view_page.php?idx=169495&part_idx=340
23. http://www.kado.net/?mod=news&act=articleView&idxno=843425
24. http://www.kyeongin.com/main/view.php?key=20170313010004397
25. http://www.upkorea.net/news/articleView.html?idxno=101715
26. http://www.daejeontoday.com/news/articleView.html?idxno=446680
27. http://www.veritas-a.com/news/articleView.html?idxno=76284
28. http://www.joongdo.co.kr/jsp/article/article_view.jsp?pq=201703132854
29. http://www.imaeil.com/sub_news/sub_news_view.php?news_id=11729&yy=2017

30. http://www.kpanews.co.kr/article/show.asp?idx=181908&table=article&category=C
31. http://view.asiae.co.kr/news/view.htm?idxno=2017031311055538148
32. http://www.asiatoday.co.kr/view.php?key=20170313010007921
33. http://www.viva100.com/main/view.php?key=20170313010004478
34. http://www.jeonmin.co.kr/news/articleView.html?idxno=166257
35. http://www.yonhapnews.co.kr/bulletin/2017/03/13/0200000000AKR20170313069800371.HTML?input=1195m
36. http://news.chosun.com/site/data/html_dir/2017/03/13/2017031300159.html
37. http://www.kyeongin.com/main/view.php?key=20170302010000580
38. http://hellodd.com/?md=news&mt=view&pid=61029
39. http://news1.kr/articles/?2933843
40. http://www.idaegu.com/?c=2&uid=359497
41. http://view.asiae.co.kr/news/view.htm?idxno=2017031219240713371
42. http://www.gukjenews.com/news/articleView.html?idxno=668150
43. http://www.gukjenews.com/news/articleView.html?idxno=668138
44. http://news.unn.net/news/articleView.html?idxno=170682
45. http://www.yonhapnews.co.kr/bulletin/2017/03/10/0200000000AKR20170310175200371.HTML?input=1195m
46. http://www.gukjenews.com/news/articleView.html?idxno=667639
47. http://www.viva100.com/main/view.php?key=20170309010003078
48. http://view.asiae.co.kr/news/view.htm?idxno=2017030916055048594
49. http://www.focus.kr/view.php?key=2017030900101943817
50. http://www.hkbs.co.kr/?m=bbs&bid=local3&uid=419025

References

Act on the Employment, etc. of Foreign Workers. Oekukin geunrojaui goyong deunge kwanhan beopryul. Retrieved from http://www.law.go.kr/lsInfoP.do?lsiSeq=206727&efYd=20190716#0000.

Act on the Immigration and Legal Status of Overseas Koreans. Jeoedongpoui choolipgookkwa beopjeok jiwie kwanhan beopryul. Retrieved from http://www.law.go.kr/lsInfoP.do?lsiSeq=213807&efYd=20200204#0000

Allport, G. W. (1954). *The nature of prejudice*. Reading, MA: Addison-Wesley Publishing Company.

Amin-Khan, T. (2012). New orientalism, securitisation and the western medias incendiary racism. *Third World Quarterly*, *33*(9), 1595–1610.

Aquino, K. (2016). Anti-racism "from below": Exploring repertoires of everyday anti-racism. *Ethnic and Racial Studies*, *39*(1), 105–122.

Awad, I. (2012). Desperately constructing ethnic audiences: Anti-immigration discourses and minority audience research in the Netherlands. *European Journal of Communication*, *28*(2), 168–182.

Banks, J. A. (1993). Multicultural education: Historical development, dimensions, and practice. *Review of Research in Education*, *19*, 3–49.

Barry, K. (1995). *The prostitution of sexuality*. New York, NY: New York University Press.

Blumberg, R. L. (1988). A general theory of gender stratification. *Sociological Theory*, 2, 23–103.

Blumer, H. (1958). Race prejudice as a sense of group position. *Pacific Sociological Review*, *1*(1), 3–7.

Bourdieu, P. (1990). *The logic of practice*. Stanford, CA: Stanford University Press

Brameld, T. (1945). Intergroup education in certain school systems. *Harvard Educational Review*, *15*(2), 93–98.

Buffett, P. (2013, July). The charitable industrial complex. *The New York Times*. Retrieved from http://www.nytimes.com/

Butler, J (1988). Performative acts and gender constitution: An essay in phenomenology and feminist theory. *Theatre Journal*, *40*(4), 519–531.

Butler, J. (1990). *Gender trouble*. New York, NY: Routledge.

Byun, H. J. (2001). *The foreign worker situation and the Old Testament interpretation*. Unpublished master's thesis. Hanil Presbyterian Seminary College, Wanju.

Campani, G. (1998). Trafficking for sexual exploitation and the sex business in the new context of international migration: The case of Italy. *South European Society & Politics*, *3*(3), 230–261.

Cha, M. K. (2010). Discussion of the article "The President Lee Myung-bak's policy on marriage migrant women and its challenges." In JCMK (Ed.), *Migration policy under President Lee Myung-bak: Is it acceptable? An analysis and recommendation* (pp. 5–15). Seoul: Joint Committee with Migrant Workers in Korea (JCMK).

Chafetz, J. S. (1997). Feminist theory and sociology: Underutilized contributions for mainstream theory. *Annual Review of Sociology*, *23*, 97–120.

Cheng, S. L. (2000). Assuming manhood: Prostitution and patriotic passions in Korea. *East Asia*, *18*(4), 40–78.

Cho, D. H. (2001). *Ijunodongundong yaksawa pyungga* [*A brief history and analysis of migrant labor movement*]. Political Studies Research. Seoul: Migrant Worker Headquarter (MWSH) for Achieving Complete Labor Rights and Actualizing Freedom of Movement and Employment.

Cho, Y. S. (2010). *The ratification and reservation of CEDAW*. International Women's Rights Project. British Columbia: Centre for Global Studies, University of Victoria.

Choo, H. Y. (2013). The cost of rights: Migrant women, feminist advocacy, and gendered morality in South Korea. *Gender and Society*, *27*(4), 445–468.

Chosunilbo. (2012, January). Multicultural children still face discrimination. Retrieved from http://english.chosun.com/site/data/html_dir/2012/01/11/2012011101030.html.

Chung, B. H. (2008). Between defector and migrant: Identities and strategies of North Koreans in South Korea. *Korean Studies*, *32*, 1–27.

Chung, Y. S. (2012). The possibility of beautiful solidarity between Korea's labor movement and migrant workers. *Homo Migrans*, *5*(6), 65–84.

Chung, Y. S. (2014). The trajectory of KCTU's policy changes regarding migrant workers. In KCTU (Ed.), *Ijunodongja nojojojikhwa sarae yeongu* [*A study of migrant worker trade union organizing experiences*] (pp. 8–16). Seoul, Korea: KCTU.

Davis, A. Y. (1996). Gender, class, and multiculturalism: Rethinking race politics. In A. F. Gordon & C. Newfield (Eds.), *Mapping multiculturalism* (pp. 40–48). Minneapolis, MN: University of Minnesota Press.

Davis-Du Bois, R. (1939). Peace and intercultural education. *Journal of Educational Sociology*, *12*(7), 418–424.

De Los Reyes, P. (2001). Women and migrants: Continuity and change in patterns of female migration in Latin America. In P. Sharpe (Ed.), *Women, gender and migration: Historical and global perspectives* (pp. 275–289. London: Routledge.

Dennison, J., & Geddes, A. (2019). A rising tide? The salience of immigration and the rise of anti-immigration political parties in Western Europe. *The Political Quarterly*, *90*(1), 107–116.

Diamond, S. (1996). Right-wing politics and the anti-immigration cause. *Social Justice*, *23*(3), 154–168.

Eckelberry, R. H. (1945). Intercultural education. *Educational Research Bulletin*, *24*(9), 229–230.

Enloe, C. (1989). Bananas, beaches and bases: Making feminist sense of international politics. Berkeley, CA: University of California Press.

Fields, G. S. (1994). Migration transition in Asia. *Asian and Pacific Migration Journal*, *3*(1), 7–30.

Flowers, R., & Swan, E. (2012). Eating the Asian other? Pedagogies of food multiculturalism in Australia. *Portal*, *9*(2), 1–30.

Giddens, A. (1984). *The constitution of society*. Berkeley, CA: University of California Press.

Giles, H. H., Pitkin, V. E., & Ingram, T. (1946). Problems of intercultural education. *Review of Educational Research*, *16*(1), 39–45.

Gilroy, P. (1990). The end of anti-racism. *New Community*, *17*(1), 71–83.

Glazer, N. (1975). *Affirmative discrimination: Ethnic inequality and public policy*. Cambridge, MA: Harvard University Press.

Glazer, N. (1997). *We are all multiculturalists now*. Cambridge, MA: Harvard University Press.

Hage, G. (2016). Recalling anti-racism. *Ethnic and Racial Studies*, *39*(1), 123–133.

Hager, D. J. (1956). New problems in intercultural education. *Journal of Educational Sociology*, *30*(4), 162–167.

Han, K. Y. (2010). The President Lee Myung-Bak's policy on marriage migrant women and its challenges. In *Migration policy under President Lee Myung-bak: Is it acceptable?*

An analysis and recommendation. Seoul: Joint Committee with Migrant Workers in Korea (JCMK).

Hanlon, H. J., & Diamond, S. (1945). What the schools can do in intercultural education. *The English Journal*, *34*(1), 32–38.

Hardy, J., & Fitzgerald, I. (2010). Negotiating 'solidarity' and internationalism: The response of Polish trade unions to migration. *Industrial Relations Journal*, *41*(4), 367–381.

Harzig, C. (2001). Women migrants as global and local agents: New research strategies on gender and migration. In P. Sharpe (Ed.), *Women, gender, and labour migration: Historical and global perspectives* (pp. 15–28). London: Routledge

Hinderliter O. D. (2009). Social studies teachers' reflections on citizenship education in Bavaria, Germany. *Race/Ethnicity: Multidisciplinary Global Contexts*, *2*(2), 189–214.

Hirose, A., & Phi, K. K. (2011). No Asians working here: Racialized otherness and authenticity in gastronomical orientalism. *Ethnic and Racial Studies*, *34*(9), 1482–1501.

Hochschild, A. R. (2003). *The commercialization of intimate life: Notes from home and work*. Berkeley, CA: University of California Press.

Hong, J. (2018). Effects of ethnic identity on the relationship between mental health and perceived discrimination among ethnic return migrants: The case of Korean Chinese return-migrated to South Korea. *Journal of Immigrant and Minority Health*, *21*, 522–532.

Hong, W. P. (2010). Multicultural education in Korea: Its development, remaining issues, and global implications. *Asia Pacific Education Review*, *11*(3), 387–395.

Honig, B. (1998). Women in the informal sector of the economy. In N. P. Stromquist (Ed.), *Women in the Third World: An encyclopedia of contemporary issues* (pp. 283–290). New York, NY: Garland Publishing, Inc.

Howe, W. A., & Lisi, P. L. (2013). *Becoming a multicultural educator: Developing awareness, gaining skills, and taking action*. Thousand Oaks, CA: Sage Publications.

International Organization for Migration (IOM). (2002). *A review of data on trafficking in the republic of Korea*. IOM Migration Research Series. Geneva: IOM.

Jeffreys, S. (1999). Globalizing sexual exploitation: Sex tourism and the traffic in women. *Leisure Studies*, *18*(3),179–196.

Johansson, J. (2014). Swedish employers and trade unions, labor migration and the welfare state: Perspectives on Swedish labor migration policy debates during the 1960s and the 2000s. *Nordic Journal of Working Life Studies*, *4*(1), 97–118.

Joint Committee with Migrants in Korea (JCMK). (2000). *Oekukin Sahnupkisoolyeonsoosaeng Inkwonbaekseo* [*White paper on the human rights of foreign industrial technical trainees*]. Seoul: JCMK.

Kang, S. U. (2015). Sahngdahmhyunjangeseo barabon damunhwagajokui wigi [A counseling-center view on the challenges of multicultural families]. Paper presented at the Seoul Counseling Center for Migrant Women Second Year Anniversary Symposium, Seoul.

Kangaspunta, K. (2003). Mapping the inhuman trade: Preliminary findings of the database on trafficking in human beings. *Forum on Crime and Society*, *3*(1–2), 81–103.

Kaplan, A., & Pease, D. (1994). *Cult of imperialism*. Durham, NC: Duke University Press.

Kilpatrick, W. H., Stone, W. J., & Cole, S. G. (1949). A frame of reference for intercultural education. *Journal of Educational Sociology*, *22*(9), 555–572.

Kim, B. H. (2018). *Iju Koroyinui Seoul Jeongchakul Uihan Daechek* [*A plan for Koryoin's settlement in Seoul*]. Seoul: The Seoul Institute.

Kim, D. (2011). Catalysers in the promotion of migrants' rights: Church-based NGOs in South Korea. *Journal of Ethnic and Migration Studies*, *37*(10), 1649–1667.

Kim, H. S. (1998). Ghimhaesung moksa (hankukoekukinnodongjajiwonsentuh daepyo) – geudeulegye jinjeong pilyohan gun doni ahnin bokgeumipnida [The Reverend Kim Hae-Sung (The director of the Foreign Worker Support Center in Korea) – They need gospel, not money]. Retrieved from https://cafe.naver.com/preaching21?iframe_url=/ArticleRead.nhn%3Fclubid=19985608%26page=1%26inCafeSearch=true%26searchBy=0%26query=%B1%E8%C7%D8%BC%BA%26includeAll=%26exclude=%26include=%26exact=%26searchdate=all%26media=0%26sortBy=date%26articleid=179%26referrerAllArticles=true

Kim, J. (2003). Insurgency and advocacy: Unauthorized foreign workers and civil society in South Korea. *Asian and Pacific Migration Journal*, *12*(3), 237–269.

Kim, J. K. (1996). An international labour migration to developing countries in Asia: A case study of Korea. *Korea Journal of Population and Development (Development & Society)*, *25*(2), 287–332.

Kim, J. K. (2005). State, civil society and international norms: Expanding the political and labor rights of foreigners in South Korea. *Asian and Pacific Migration Journal*, *14*(4), 383–418.

Kim, J. K. (2009). Ijuminkwa kŏn'gang: Han'guk-esŏ mitŭngnok ijuminŭi pogŏnŭiryosŏbisŭ chŏpkŭnsŏngi pojangtoeŏya hanŭn'ga? [Migrants and health: Should unauthorized migrants have access to healthcare in Korea?]. In WeFriends Aid (Ed.), *Han'guksahoewa Ijuminkŏn'gang: oeguginnodongja ŭiryopaeksŏ* 2 [Korean Society and Migrant Health: The White Papers on the Migrant Worker Health 2], (pp. 277–296). Seoul: *ch'ŏngnyŏn ŭisa*.

Kim, J. K. (2011). The politics of culture in multicultural Korea. *Journal of Ethnic and Migration Studies*, *37*(10), 1583–1604.

Kim, J. K. (2014). The third-order multiculturalism: Civil rights, diversity, and equality in Korea's multicultural education. *Asia Pacific Education Review*, *15*, 401–408.

Kim, J. K. (2015). Embedded solidarity: International migrant labor advocacy in South Korea. In J. A. Vallejo (Ed.), *Immigration and work: Research in the sociology of work* (pp. 75–98). Bingley: Emerald Group Publishing Limited.

Kim, J. K., & Fu, M. (2008). International women in South Korea's sex industry: A new commodity frontier. *Asian Survey*, *48*(3), 492–513.

Kim, J. U., & Jang, D. J. (2007). Aliens among brothers? The status and perception of North Korean refugees in South Korea. *Asian Perspective*, *31*(2), 5–22.

Kim, M. (2013). Citizenship projects for marriage migrants in South Korea: Intersecting motherhood with ethnicity and class. *Social Politics*, *20*(4), 455–481.

Kim, N. H. J. (2016). Introduction: Co-ethnics, refugees, or immigrants? Multiple identities of North Koreans in 'multicultural' South Korea. *Asian Ethnicity*, *17*(2), 167–170.

Kim, S., & Kim, L. H. R. (2012). The need for multicultural education in South Korea. In D. Urias (Ed.), *The Immigration and Education Nexus* (pp. 243–251). Rotterdam: Sense Publishers.

Kipling, R. (1899). The white man's burden. *McClure's Magazine*, February. Retrieved from http://www.unz.org/Pub/McClures-1899feb-00290.

Ko, G. A. (2019). Ijunodongja myungdongsungdang soesaseul nongsung: hyundaepan noyedeului soesaseul hahmsung, geurobutuh palnyun [Migrant worker protest at Myungdong Cathedral: Voices of the modern-day slaves, 8 years after]. Retrieved from https://www.sarangbang.or.kr/hrdailynews/66892.

Kohli, R. (2008). Breaking the cycle of racism in the classroom: Critical race reflections from future teachers of color. *Teacher Education Quarterly*, *35*(4), 177–188.

Koo, H. (2002). *Korean workers: The culture and politics of class formation*. Ithaca, NY: Cornell University Press.

Korea Institute of Criminology (KIC). (2002a). *Songmaemae Shilt'ae Mit Kyongjaegyumo-e Kwanhan Chon-gukchosa* [*A national study on the actual condition and the economic scope of the sex industry*]. Seoul: Korean Institute of Criminology.

Korea Institute of Criminology (KIC). (2002b). *Songchakchwi Mokjeokui Inshinmaemae Hyunhwangkwa Bupjeok Daeungbangan [Stopping traffic: exploring the realities of and responses to trafficking in women for sexual exploitation in Korea]*. Seoul: Korean Institute of Criminology.

Korean Institute of Criminology (KIC). (2011). *A Review of Problems and Solutions Related to International Human Trafficking: Focus on Korea, Russia and the Commonwealth of Independent States* (CIS). Seoul: Korean Institute of Criminology.

Korea Labor Institute. (2007). *Oekukinryuk nodongsijang bunseok mit jungjangki kwanlichege gaeseonbanghyang yeongu [A study of foreign labor market analysis and the mid-term assessment of the management system]*. Seoul: Korea Labor Institute.

Korea Labor Welfare Corporation. (2003). *Employment insurance collection and industrial accident compensation insurance data and analysis*. Seoul: Korea Labor Welfare Corporation.

Korea Research Institute for Workers' Human Rights and Justice. (1995). Policies and protective measures concerning foreign workers in Asia and Europe. Paper presented at the international seminar on Policy and Protection for Migrant Workers in Asia and Europe, organized jointly by Friedrich-Ebert-Stiftung and the Korea Research Institute for Workers' Human Rights and Justice, May 30–31, Seoul.

Korea Women Development Institute (KWDI). (2004). *Chabyule daehan gukminuishik mit suyongseong yeongu [A Study on public perception of and receptivity to discrimination]*. Seoul: Korea Women Development Institute.

Korean Confederation of Trade Unions (KCTU). (2000). *Johapwon uishik mit senghwalsiltae josa [A study of union member attitudes and living conditions, 1999]*. A summary report of the results. Seoul: KCTU.

Korean Confederation of Trade Unions (KCTU). (2002a). *Ijunodongja gwanryun ipbeopae daehahn minjunochong jeongchekbanghyang [KCTU policy direction regarding migrant worker related laws]*. Policy report. Seoul: KCTU.

Korean Confederation of Trade Unions (KCTU). (2002b). Legislative public hearing on foreign worker employment and securing basic rights, sponsored by Lawyers for a Democratic Society (minbyun), Ministry of Health and Welfare, and Korean Confederation of Trade Unions (KCTU), National Assembly, July 12, 2002.

Korean Confederation of Trade Unions (KCTU). (2014). *Ijunodongja nojojojikhwa sarae yeongu [A study of migrant worker trade union organizing experiences]*. Seoul: KCTU.

Kymlicka, W. (2010). The rise and fall of multiculturalism? New debates on inclusion and accommodation in diverse societies. *International Social Science Journal, 61*, 97–112.

Lacovetta, F., Quinlan, M., & Radforth, I. (1996). Immigration and labour: Australia and Canada compared. *Labour/Le Travail, 38*(71), 90–115.

Lee, B. H. (2015). Changing cross-movement coalitions between labor unions and civil society organizations in South Korea. *Development and Society, 44*(2), 199–218.

Lee, H. K. (2003). Gender, migration and civil activism in South Korea. *Asian and Pacific Migration Journal, 12*(1–2), 127–154.

Lee, K. Y. C. (2001). Yeoseongijunodongjaui inkwoneul uihan hwaldong [Activities pertaining to migrant women workers' human rights]. Paper presented at the 2001 International Citizens' Forum on Foreign Migrant Workers, Seoul.

Lee, S., & Chien, Y. C. (2017). The making of 'skilled' overseas Koreans: Transformation of visa policies for co-ethnic migrants in South Korea. *Journal of Ethnic and Migration Studies, 43*(3), 2193–2210.

Lee, S. H. (1993). Transitional politics in Korea, 1987–1992: Activation of civil society. *Pacific Affairs, 66*(3), 351–367.

Lee, S. J., & Walsh, D. (2015). Teaching (in)justice: One teacher's work with immigrant English learners. *Urban Review, 47*(1), 45–66.

Lee, S. S. (2006). Feminism and preventive act of prostitution: Can sex worker speak? *Discourse 201*, *9*(2), 107–138.

Lee, Y. J. (2001). *Nodongundongeuro geodeupnaneun ijunodongundongui jeongchijeok jojikjeok gwaje* [*Overcoming migrant labor movement's political and organization challenge through labor movement*]. Political Studies Research. Seoul: Migrant Worker Headquarter (MWSH) for Achieving Complete Labor Rights and Actualizing Freedom of Movement and Employment.

Lee, Y. J. (2014). An experience of Migrant Worker Headquarter, Equality Trade Union: Migrant Worker Division: The rise of migrant worker movement within labor movement. In KCTU (Ed.), *Ijunodongja nojojojikhwa sarae yeongu* [*A study of migrant worker trade union organizing experiences*] (pp. 17–33). Seoul: KCTU.

Lim, S. H. (2015). *Bulbeop cheryu oegukingeunrojaui nojo gyulseong ganeung pangyului uimiwa sisajeom* [*A meaning and perspective regarding the decision to allow unauthorized workers to form labor unions*]. Issue and Perspective [*ishuwa nonjeom*], 14 July. Seoul: Legislative Research Unit of the National Assembly.

Matsui, Y. (1999). Women in the new Asia. Bangkok: White Lotus

McGill, C. (2003). *Human traffic: Sex, slaves and immigration*. London: Vision Paperbacks.

Medical Network. (2002). *Workshop for foreign worker medical network*. Seoul: Yonsei University.

Mies, M. (1998). *Patriarchy and accumulation on a world-scale: Women in the international division of labor*. London: Zed Books Ltd.

Miller, H. (1969). Social work in the black ghetto: The new colonialism. *Social Work*, *14*(3), 65–76.

Ministry of Education and Human Resources Development. (2006). *Yuahreul wihan Segye Ihae mit Damunhwagyoyook [Multicultural and global education for children*. Seoul: Ministry of Education and Human Resources Development.

Ministry of Education and Human Resources Development. (2007). *Damunhwagajeong Janyo Gyoyook jiwon Daechek* [*A plan to support the children of multicultural families*]. Seoul: Ministry of Education and Human Resources Development.

Ministry of Education, Science and Technology. (2008). *Icheonpalnyundo Damunhwagajeong Haksaeng Gyoyook Jiwon Gyehoek* [*A plan to support the children of multicultural families for the year 2008*]. Seoul: Ministry of Education, Science and Technology.

Ministry of Foreign Affairs. (various years). *Status of overseas Koreans*. Seoul: Ministry of Foreign Affairs.

Ministry of Gender Equality. (2004). *Oekukyeosung sungmeme shiltejosa* [*Research on the status of foreign sex workers*]. Seoul: Korea Culture and Tourism Policy Institute.

Ministry of Justice. (2015). *Tonggyeyonboro boneun choolipkuk oekukin jeongchek* [*Policies regarding foreigners through the lens of annual statistical data*]. Korea: Ministry of Justice.

Ministry of Justice. Immigration Policy Commission. (2012). *The 2nd basic plan of immigration policy: 2013–2017*. Seoul: Ministry of Justice.

Ministry of Justice. Korea Immigration Service (KIS). (2016). *Kyulhoniminja mit gwihwaja janyo hyunhwang* [*Children of marriage migrants and naturalized citizens in Korea*]. Korea: Ministry of Justice.

Ministry of Justice. Korea Immigration Service (KIS). (2018a). *Combined statistics of immigration and resident foreigners*. Seoul: Ministry of Justice.

Ministry of Justice. Korea Immigration Service (KIS). (2018b). *Korean heritage with foreign nationality*. Seoul: Ministry of Justice.

Ministry of Justice. Korea Immigration Service (KIS). (2018c). *Korean nationality recovery, naturalization, renunciation, and loss*. Seoul: Ministry of Justice.

Ministry of Labor. (2007). *Employment system for foreign workers of the Republic of Korea*. Seoul: Ministry of Labor.

Ministry of Unification. (2019). *Number of North Korean defectors entering South Korea*. Seoul: Ministry of Justice.

Moon, K. H. S. (2007). Resurrecting prostitutes and overturning treaties: Gender politics in the "anti-American" movement in South Korea. *Journal of Asian Studies*, *66*(1), 129–157.

Moon, K. H. S. (2014). South Korean civil society organizations, human rights norms, and North Korea. *Critical Asian Studies*, *46*(1), 65–89.

Myrdal, G. (1944). *An American dilemma: The negro problem and modern democracy*. New York: Harper & Bros.

North Korean Refugees Protection and Settlement Support Act. (1997). Bookhan Italjoominui boho mit jeongchakjiwone kwanhan beopryul. Retrieved from http://www.law.go.kr/lsInfoP.do?lsiSeq=206648#0000.

O'Connell Davidson, J. (1998). *Prostitution, power and freedom*. Ann Arbor, MI: University of Michigan Press.

Olneck, M. R. (2011). Facing multiculturalism's challenges in Korean education and society. *Asia Pacific Education Review*, *12*(4), 675–690.

Overseas Koreans Foundation Act. (1997). Jewe dongpo jedanbeop. Retrieved from https://elaw.klri.re.kr/eng_mobile/viewer.do?hseq=35126&type=part&key=44

Paris, D. (2012). Culturally sustaining pedagogy: A needed change in stance, terminology, and practice. *Educational Researcher*, *41*(3), 93–97.

Park, C. U. (2019). Hangukgyohoeui ijuminseonkyo yoksakwa hyanghu kwaje. [A history of Korean church's migrant mission and the future work]. Retrieved from https://cafe.naver.com/historicaljesus/11.

Park, G. C., & Watson, S. L. (2011). Multicultural education in Korea. *Multicultural Education*, *19*(3) 1–5.

Park, K. H. (2002). *The church's teachings pertaining to foreign worker issues*. Unpublished master's thesis. Taegu Catholic University, Taegu.

Park, S. W. (1996). Hankukne ijunodongja jiwonhwaldong [Migrant advocacy activities in Korea]. Paper presented at the Asian Migrant Center, Hong Kong, September 19, 1996.

Park, S. W. (2002). Oegukinijunodongja tujengui jeongaewa jeongbujeongchekui munjejeom [Progress of migrant worker movement and government policy issues]. Retrieved from http://www.inkwon.or.kr/maybbs/view.php?db=inkwon&code=data7&n=41.

Park, S. W. (2010). Yokdae jeongbuui ijujeongchek byunhwawa minganui daeung. [Changes in government policies on immigration and the civil society responses]. In *President Lee Myung-bak government's immigration policy, is it acceptable*? Policy discussion. National Human Rights Commission of Korea, May 13, sponsored by the Joint Committee with Migrant Workers in Korea.

Park, Y. B. (1994). The turning point in international labor migration and economic development in Korea. *Asian and Pacific Migration Journal*, *3*(1), 149–174.

Piper, N. (2003). Feminization of labor migration as violence against women. *Violence Against Women*, *9*(6), 723–745.

Pitcher, B. (2009). The global politics of multiculturalism. *Development*, *52*(4), 456–459.

Portes, A. (1978). Migration and underdevelopment. *Politics and Society*, *8*(1), 11–48.

Portice, J., & Reicher, S. (2018). Arguments for European disintegration: A mobilization analysis of anti-immigration speeches by U.K. political leaders. *Political Psychology*, *39*(6), 1357–1372.

PSCORE. (2015). *North Korean workers overseas: State-sponsored slavery*. A preliminary report submitted to the 28th session of the UN HRC. Seoul: PSCORE.

Ra, D. C. (2014). Gowi gongjikjadeul nobles oblijoo maja? Yoengan 100 manwon isang gibuja gyeowu 18 myung bulgwa [Are the high officials in Korea practicing nobles oblige? Only 18 officials donated over 100,000 won], April. The Kukmin Ilbo. Retrieved from http://news.kmib.co.kr/.

Rondilla, J., & Spickard, P. (2007). *Is lighter better? Skin-tone discrimination among Asian Americans*. New York, NY: Rowman and Littlefield Publishers, Inc.

Rooduijn, M. (2015). The rise of the populist radical right in Western Europe. *European View*, *14*, 3–11.

Sacks, K. (1974). Engels revisited: Women, the organization of production, and private property. In M. Z. Rosaldo & L. Lamphere (Eds.), *Woman, culture, and society* (pp. 207–222). Stanford, CA: Stanford University Press.

Said, E. W. (2003). *Orientalism*. New York, NY: Vintage Books.

Sassen-Koob, S. (1981). Towards a conceptualization of immigrant labor. *Social Problems*, *29*(1), 65–85.

Seok, W. J. (2003). *Ijunodongja munjewa hankooksahoeui gwaje*. [*The foreign worker-related problems and the challenges of the Korean society*]. Seoul: Association for Foreign Workers Human Rights.

Seol, D. H. (2000). A plan for introducing and implementing foreign worker Employment Permit System. In JCMK (Ed.), *Informal gatherings for a better foreign worker system* (pp. 12–20). Seoul: JCMK.

Shapiro, M. J. (1997). Narrating the nation, unwelcoming the stranger: Anti-immigration policy in contemporary America. *Alternatives: Global, Local, Political*, *22*(1), 1–34.

Shelton, B. A., & Agger, B. (1993). Shotgun wedding, unhappy marriage, no-fault divorce? Rethinking the feminism-Marxism relationship. In E. England (Ed.), *Theory on gender/feminism on theory* (pp. 25–41). New York, NY: Aldine De Grutyer.

Skrobanek, S., Boonpakdi, N., & Janthakeero, C. (1997). *The traffic in women: Human realities of the international sex trade*. London: Zed Books Ltd.

Sleeter, C. E. (1996). Multicultural education as a social movement. *Theory into Practice*, *35*(4), 239–247.

Small and Medium Business Administration (SMBA). (2002). *Guide for foreign industrial trainee system implementation*. Seoul: Small and Medium Business Administration.

So, R. M. (2007). Kukjegyeolhon ijuyeoseongui inkwon siltewa gwanryeon beopjeok jengjeom [Key points of human rights conditions and laws pertaining to international women marriage migrants]. Paper presented at the Seoul national university institute for gender research conference, November, Seoul.

Soh, C. S. (2004). Women's sexual labor and state in Korean history. *Journal of Women's History*, *15*(4), 170–177.

Sokoloff, N. (1980). *Between Money and Love: The Dialectics of Women's Home and Market Work*. New York: Praeger.

Song, C. (2014). Identity politics and the meaning of homeland among Korean Chinese migrants in South Korea. *Urban Anthropology and Studies of Cultural Systems and World Economic Development*, *43*(4), 441–479.

Song, H. K. (1999). *Labor unions in the Republic of Korea: Challenge and choice*. Discussion Papers, Labour and Society Programme.International Institute for Labour Studies, International Labour Organization, Geneva.

Song, J. H. (2006). Oekukin nodongja jiwondancheui hyunhwanggwa hwaldong [Assessment and activities of foreign labor support organizations]. *Minjokyeongu*, *28*, 29–53.

Special Act to Support the Residency Acquisition of Koreans in the Former Soviet Union Countries (Koryoin Compatriot Act). (2010). Goryoindongpo hapbeopjeok cheryujagyuk chwideuk mit jeongchak jiwoneul uihan teukbyulbeop. Retrieved from http://www.law.go.kr/lsInfoP.do?lsiSeq=136662&efYd=20130323#0000

Statistics Korea. (2014). Gyulhoniminja gibonhyunhwang [Basic information pertaining to marriage migrants]. Retrieved from http://www.index.go.kr/potal/main/EachDtlPageDetail.do?idx_cd=2819.

Stolzenberg, N. M. (2002). The return of the repressed: Illiberal groups in a liberal state liberalism and illiberalism. *Journal of Contemporary Legal Issues*, *12*(2), 897–940.

Summerfield, G., & Aslanbeigui, N. (1998). The impact of structural adjustment and economic reform on women. In N. P. Stromquist (Ed.), *Women in the third world: An encyclopedia of contemporary issues* (pp. 332–340). New York, NY: Garland Publishing, Inc.

Taba, H., & Van Til, W. (1945). *Democratic human relations: Promising practices in intergroup and intercultural education in the social studies*. Washington, DC: Department of the National Education Association.

UN Committee on the Elimination of Discrimination Against Women (CEDAW). (2010). Korea Women's Associations United (KWAU). *Critical issues on the seventh periodical report on the convention on the elimination of all forms of discrimination against women*.

UN Committee on the Elimination of Discrimination Against Women (CEDAW). (2011). Korea Women's Associations United (KWAU). *An examination of the seventh periodic report by the Republic of Korea (2006–2009) on the implementation of the UN Convention on the elimination of all forms of discrimination against women*. NGO Shadow Report, Republic of Korea, Korea.

UN Committee on the Elimination of Discrimination Against Women (CEDAW). (2017). Korea Women's Associations United (KWAU). *Republic of Korea: Submission to the Committee on the Elimination of Discrimination against Women (CEDAW Committee) for the adoption of the list of issues*. Pre-sessional working group of the 69th session, July 24–28.

UN Committee on the Elimination of Discrimination Against Women (CEDAW). (2018). Korea Women's Associations United (KWAU). *Concerns and recommendations on the Republic of Korea*. NGO Submission to CEDAW, 69th Session, February 19–March 9.

Van Heerden, S., De Lange, S. L., Van der Brug, W., & Fennema, M. (2014). The immigration and integration debate in the Netherlands: Discursive and programmatic reactions to the rise of anti-immigration parties. *Journal of Ethnic and Migration Studies*, *40*(1), 119–136.

Vickery, W. E. & Cole, S. G. (1943). *Intercultural education in American schools: Proposed objectives and methods*. New York, NY: Harper and Brothers Publishers.

Wark, C., & Galliher, J. F. (2007). Emory Bogardus and the origins of the social distance scale. *American Sociologist*, *38*, 383–395.

Watanabe, S. (1994). The Lewisian turning point in international labor migration: The case of Japan. *Asian and Pacific Migration Journal*, *3*(1), 119–148.

Weekly Donga. (2003). A Centerpiece of citizens movement: The '3rd generation leader.' *Weekly Donga*, August. Retrieved from http://weekly.donga.com/3/all/11/70700/1

Wells, K. M. (Ed.). (1995). *South Korea's minjung movement: The culture and politics of dissidence*. Honolulu: University of Hawaii Press.

West, C., & Fenstermaker, S. (1995). Doing difference. *Gender and Society*, *9*, 8–37.

Wiggen, M. (2012). Rethinking anti-immigration rhetoric after the Oslo and Utoya terror attacks. *New Political Science*, *34*(4), 585–604.

Williams, R. (1989). *Resources of hope: Culture, democracy, socialism*. London: Verso.

Won, H. Y. (2016, February). Seolgigan oekukin bumjoe puripobatda [Uprooted foreigner crime during the New Year break]. Retrieved from http://news.heraldcorp.com/

Yoon, I. J. (2005). *Jangrae urinara Inryuknan moonje haegyul mit jewedongpo inryuk hwalyongbangan* [*A study on addressing the nation's future labor shortage and the utilization of overseas Korean labor*]. Final Report Submitted to the Ministry of Justice. Seoul: Ministry of Justice.

Yoon, W. H. (1995) Foreign worker protection policies and the role of trade unions. Paper presented at the international seminar on Policy and Protection for Migrant Workers in Asia and Europe, organized jointly by Friedrich-Ebert-Stiftung and the Korea Research Institute for Workers' Human Rights and Justice, May 30–31, Seoul.

Zolberg, A. R. (1979). International migration policies in a changing world system. In W. H. McNeill & R. Adams (Eds.), *Human migration: Patterns and policies* (pp. 241–248). Bloomington, IN: Indiana University Press.

Index

Note: Page numbers followed by "*n*" indicate notes.

Printed and bound by CPI Group (UK) Ltd, Croydon, CR0 4YY
13/09/2026
14961028-0008